Major Business and Technology Trends Shaping the Contemporary World

Major Business and Technology Trends Shaping the Contemporary World

K.H. Yeganeh

BEP BUSINESS EXPERT PRESS

Major Business and Technology Trends Shaping the Contemporary World

First published in 2019 by
Business Expert Press, LLC
222 East 46th Street, New York, NY 10017
www.businessexpertpress.com

ISBN-13: 978-1-63157-785-7 (paperback)
ISBN-13: 978-1-63157-786-4 (e-book)

Business Expert Press International Business Collection

Collection ISSN: 1948-2752 (print)
Collection ISSN: 1948-2760 (electronic)

Cover and interior design by Exeter Premedia Services Private Ltd., Chennai, India

First edition: 2019

10 9 8 7 6 5 4 3 2 1

Printed in the United States of America.

Abstract

The current volume relies on a wide variety of scholarly and professional resources to analyze the nature, causes, and consequences of major business and technology trends of our time. The text is organized in three parts and 11 chapters. The first part examines prospects for energy, commodities, water, food, and healthcare. The second part analyzes leading business transformations such as the sharing economy, Fourth Industrial Revolution, gig economy, and recent developments in the global economy, consumption, labor, employment, and education. The third part focuses on technological innovation and examines various advances in areas such as automation, robotics, data, connectivity, quantum computing, new materials, and energies. This book is a valuable reference for business leaders, managers, students, and all those who are passionate about understanding our rapidly changing world.

Keywords

augmented intelligence; automation; blockchain; business transformations; commodities; consumption; food; Fourth Industrial Revolution; gig economy; global economy; global innovation; healthcare; programmable materials; quantum computing; sharing economy; smart dust; nanomaterials; new energies; water scarcity

Contents

PART I

Prospects for Energy, Commodities, Water, Food, and Healthcare

CHAPTER 1

Energy, Commodities, and Water

The Surge of Energy Demand in Developing Economies

The global primary energy demand has grown 1.6 times since 1970, from 104.5 million barrels of oil equivalent (mboe/d) in 1970 to 273.9 mboe/d in 2014 and is expected to increase by another 40 percent by 2040 [8]. The most important driver of energy demand is economic growth, which is often measured in terms of the gross domestic product (GDP). The world's GDP is expected to rise by 3.3 percent per year between 2012 and 2040, suggesting a steady increase in energy demand over the course of the next three decades. The fastest rates of economic growth belong to the developing economies outside of the Organization for Economic Cooperation and Development (OECD) with a GDP growth of almost 4.2 percent per year. In the developed economies or the OECD club, the GDP will grow at a much slower rate of 2 percent per year over the course of the next three decades [1]. Energy consumption per capita in the OECD region has already peaked around 2005 and is now either stable or declining. This pattern of energy consumption in developed economies relates to service-based and technologically advanced economies that

capitalize on energy-efficiency gains [8]. The developed and rich economies still have the highest levels of energy consumption per capita, but
they are marked by more mature economies and lower levels of population growth. It is estimated that the per capita energy use in the OECD
countries is still 60 to 70 percent higher than that in the rest of the world.
For example, in the United States, energy consumption is almost 30 times
higher than in Bangladesh.

Because of a combination of higher population growth, economic
development, and changes in their lifestyles, the developing economies
will experience the highest levels of increase in energy consumption in the
next three decades. Across the world, more than 1.3 billion people still
do not have access to electricity, and 3 billion people use simple stoves
burning waste, wood, and animal dung for heating and cooking [2]. As
the least developed regions of the world undergo socio-economic development, they will necessarily add to the global energy consumption [3].
In emerging and developing economies, energy consumption per capita
is poised to increase over the course of the next three decades, reflecting greater electrification, urbanization, expansion of the middle class,
and strong economic growth [8]. According to the International Energy
Agency (IEA), non-OECD energy demand will increase by over 70 percent between 2012 and 2040 compared with a growth of 18 percent in
OECD nations [4] (see Figure 1.1). By 2020, China will surpass OECD
America in terms of real GDP, and by 2040, China's GDP will be more
than 1.5 times that of OECD America. Similarly, India will surpass the
OECD Europe around 2034, and by 2040, India's real GDP will be about
the same size as the OECD America [8]. The two Asian giants China and
India will lead the developing world in rising standards of living, GDP
growth, and an increase in energy demand. China and India together will
account for almost half the expected increase in global energy demand by
2040 [5, 1]. In addition, a group of 10 countries consisting of Brazil, Mexico, South Africa, Nigeria, Egypt, Turkey, Saudi Arabia, Iran, Thailand,
and Indonesia collectively will account for about 30 percent of the projected growth in energy demand in the next three decades [5]. According
to the U.S. Energy Information Administration, two-thirds of the world's
primary energy will be consumed in the developing economies by 2040.
This level of energy consumption in developing economies represents an

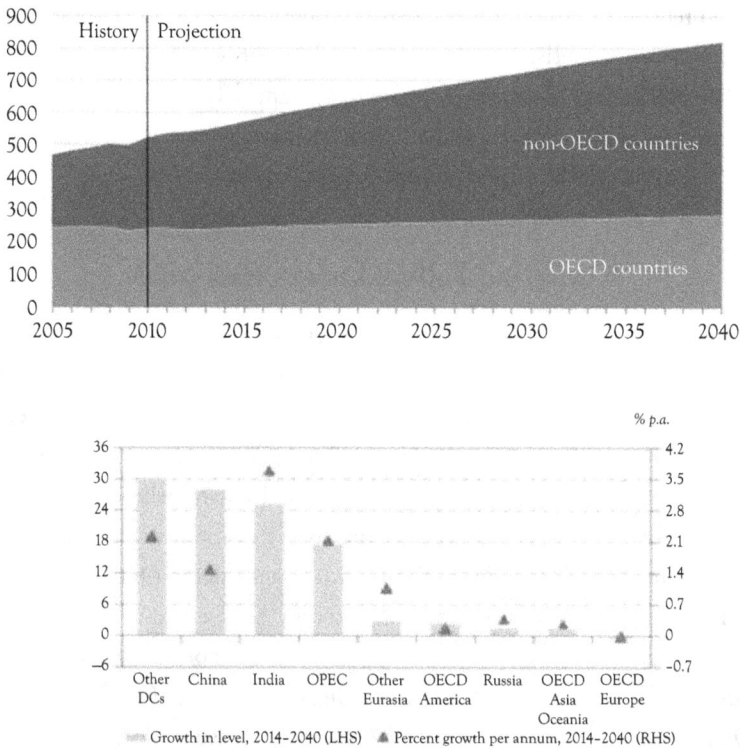

Figure 1.1 Projected world primary energy consumption until 2040

Source: [2].

increase of 54 percent from 2010's levels. By contrast, the OCED countries, including European nations, the United States, Canada, Japan, and
Australia, will experience an increase of almost 0.5 percent a year in energy
demand [6]. The global growth in energy demand is driven mainly by road
transportation, petrochemicals, and aviation sectors. As the developing
economies are significantly lagging behind the developed economies in
the number of cars per capita, they represent a huge potential for growth
in the size of the global car fleet that will clearly boost the global energy
demand [7]. The total number of passenger cars is expected to double
in only 25 years between 2015 and 2040, reaching from 1 billion to 2.1
billion [2]. Similarly, aviation demand growth is expected to accelerate in
every region of the world, but mostly in China and India. An important
remark is that many developing economies lack the required infrastructure or resources to utilize and improve energy resources efficiently and

often rely on carbon-polluting coal and other fossil fuels to generate electricity. Consequently, the world's levels of greenhouse gas emissions and other pollutants are expected to rise significantly. Unless the developing economies like China and India switch to alternative and clean energies, we can expect disastrous environmental consequences.

Rising and Falling Energy Resources

According to the IEA, the total investment in the energy sector is estimated at around 1.8 trillion U.S. dollars per year [2]. Consistent with the same estimates, a cumulative 44 trillion U.S. dollars in investment is needed in global energy supply by 2040. While almost all types of energy resources are expected to grow, renewables are believed to be the fastest-growing energy sources over the course of the next three decades (see Figure 1.2). According to the International Energy Outlook (IEO), renewable energy consumption will grow by an average of 2.6 percent per year between 2017 and 2040 [1]. After renewable energies, nuclear power is the world's second fastest-growing energy source (see Figure 1.2). Despite some serious security concerns, the consumption of nuclear energy is predicted to increase by 2.3 percent per year in the next three decades [1]. The consumption of fossil fuels has been subject to extensive

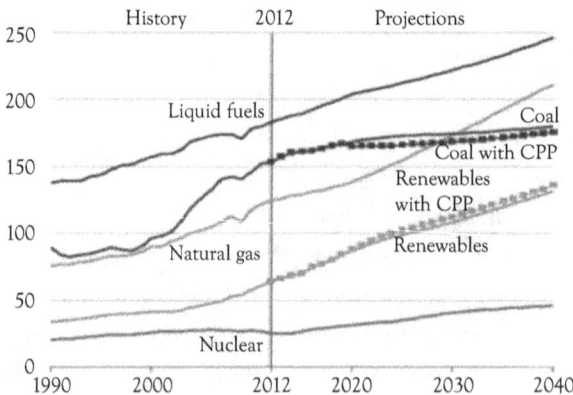

Figure 1.2 Total world energy consumption by energy source 1990–2040 (Quadrillion Btu)

Source: [1].

Note: Dotted lines for coal and renewables show projected effects of the U.S. Clean Power Plan.

criticism in the past decade, and for that reason, this source of energy may have a much slower growth rate than previously expected. Between 2014 and 2015, the fossil fuel consumption subsidies dropped from 500 billion U.S. dollars to 325 billion U.S. dollars, reflecting a significant decline in the fossil fuel development [2]. Regulations to accelerate fuel efficiency improvements and a faster penetration of alternative fuel vehicles may significantly reduce fossil fuel demand. Nevertheless, fossil fuels are expected to constitute 78 percent of the energy mix in 2040 [1]. According to the OPEC, oil and natural gas together will account for almost 53 percent of the energy needs in 2040, which is equal to the present levels [8]. Much of the demand for oil comes from the transport sector. Substitution of oil in the transport sector is happening, but it is not expected to reach more than 5 percent for the next decade [9]. Currently, several fundamental changes are affecting the oil industry, including the emergence of non-OPEC oil supply, the rise of shale oil, heavy oil, and tar sands, and increased production from mature and frontier fields [9]. According to the IEO2016 reports, the consumption of oil and other liquid fuels is expected to grow from 90 million barrels per day in 2012 to 121 million barrels per day in 2040. Traditionally, the transportation and industrial sectors are the main consumers of oil and other liquid fuels. Oil will probably remain the fuel with the largest share at least for the next two decades and eventually will be overtaken by gas around 2040 or afterward [8].

Among the fossil fuels, natural gas is the fastest-growing source of energy in the next four decades, as its consumption is supposed to increase by 1.9 percent per year [1]. Due to its adverse environmental effects, coal is recognized as the world's slowest-growing energy source. According to the IEO2016 projections, the consumption of coal is expected to grow only 0.6 percent per year by 2040. While its share in the total global energy mix is expected to decline, the overall coal consumption is expected to increase in the long term [8]. Currently, more than 7,700 million tons of coal is used by many sectors, including power generation, iron and steel production, cement manufacturing, and as a liquid fuel. It is thought provoking to note that coal fuels 40 percent of the world's electricity [9]. Despite its polluting effects, the consumption of coal will be significant mainly in China, the United States, and India, which will account for more than 70 percent of the world's coal consumption. In the face of the rapid growth of alternative energies, fossil fuels will continue to dominate the energy consumption in the next three decades. According to the IEA, the share of fossil fuels in the world energy mix has remained 82 percent, which is the same as it was 25 years ago. Based on the same estimates, fossil fuels will hardly lose ground, as their share in the global energy mix will be hovering around 75 percent by 2035.

The Attractiveness of Natural Gas

Natural gas is the only fossil fuel whose share of the primary energy mix is expected to grow in the next three decades. Natural gas represents a much cleaner source of energy than other fossil fuels such as coal and oil. In comparison with other fossil fuels, natural gas benefits from two main advantages, namely, lower production costs and environmental credentials. For instance, natural gas consumption produces lower emissions of CO_2 and other dangerous substances such as sulfur and nitrogen compounds. Furthermore, unlike nuclear power, natural gas involves lower levels of risk. As more governments are taking measures to cut carbon dioxide emissions, natural gas is expected to become the preferred source of energy. In recent years, technological advances have changed the industry and created new prospects for affordable and secure supplies of natural gas. In addition, natural gas markets have become globally interconnected because of business developments such as gas-to-gas pricing, short-term trade, and consumer bargaining power [9]. Overall, moderate capital cost, affordable pricing, low polluting effects, and a high fuel efficiency make natural gas one of the most attractive energy sources. Currently, natural gas is the number three fuel, reflecting 24 percent of the global primary energy, and it is the second energy source in power generation, representing a 22 percent share [9]. According to the IEO2016 report, global gas demand is forecast to increase on average by 2.1 percent per year from 120 trillion cubic feet in 2012 to 203 trillion cubic feet in 2040 [1]. Except for Japan, gas consumption is expected to increase everywhere across the world, particularly in China, the Middle East, and India. By 2040, China will become one of the world's largest consumers and importers of natural gas [2].

The world's natural gas supply is expected to grow by almost 70 percent by 2040. The big part of the increased supply will happen in developing economies of Asia and the Middle East, whereas the United States and Russia will witness the highest level of production increase among the developed economies. Three countries, namely, China, the United States, and Russia, will be responsible for almost 45 percent of the growth in the global production of natural gas over the next three decades. While the production of natural gas in Russia is powered by the development of new resources in the Arctic and eastern regions, in the United States, the production increase is caused by the expansion of shale resources [1]. Similarly, the trade of natural gas is expected to rapidly grow by 2040. The trade of liquefied natural gas could double in the next decades, but the trade via pipelines will account for most of the global natural gas trade, particularly in Europe, the United States, and Canada [1].

More recently, by relying on technological breakthroughs in the areas of hydraulic fracturing and directional drilling, the North American producers have succeeded to substantially increase their natural gas production. Consequently, the United States has become a major gas producer. Currently, natural gas generates more than 24 percent of U.S. electricity [10]. At existing levels of production, the U.S. resources of natural gas could last about 100 years [10]. Based on several estimates, the United States could become a net exporter of natural gas by 2020. For now, shale gas production is limited to North America, but after 2020, shale gas will become important in other parts of the world, as there are considerable reserves of shale gas in Asia and Latin America. In Asia, China is likely to acquire the required technologies and start shale gas production [7]. Nevertheless, shale gas production has been subject to criticism due to its destructive effects on the environment [11]. In addition to shale gas production, new conventional gas reserves are found in new regions of the world. This means that the other parts of the world such as South-East Africa, Asia, and the Mediterranean could become big producers of natural gas.

The Rise of Alternative and Renewable Energies in Developed and Developing Economies

Alternative and renewable energies are considered substitutes to coal, oil, and other fossil fuels. They include a variety of sources, including biomass, hydropower, geothermal, solar energy, wind energy, and wave power. In general, alternative energies can be renewed, are less pollutant, and cause no or little environmental damage. The Paris Climate Accord (adopted in 2015) called for a global reduction in emissions in order to keep global warming within 2°C above pre-industrial levels. A major consequence of the Paris Climate Accord was an unprecedented encouragement to acceleration in the shift from fossil fuels to renewable energy sources. In 2015, the global investments in renewable energies hit record levels (286 billion U.S. dollars) or the double of investments in fossil fuels (130 billion U.S. dollars), highlighting the fact that the move to renewable energies has gained considerable momentum. In Europe, quick development of renewable power generation, particularly wind and solar, has been driven by the European Union's Renewable Energy Directive and national targets [12].

A combination of factors can explain the phenomenal move to renewable energy sources, including technological breakthroughs, cost declines, new financing structures, regulatory support, governmental incentives and subsidies, and public opinion support in both developed and developing economies. In Germany, the share of renewable energy in the national gross electricity production has risen from 7 percent in 2000 to 24 percent in 2013. Because of the increasing share of renewable energies, Germany has been able to turn off several nuclear power plants in the past three years [12]. Some European countries such as Spain provide generous and unlimited subsidy schemes. For the first time, developing economies are investing more than the developed world in renewable energies [13]. In 2015, China's investment in renewable energies topped 100 billion U.S. dollars or almost one-third of the global energy investment. Other countries, including Chile, South Africa, and Mexico, have made huge investments in renewable energies. Indeed, a visible trend in renewable energies is their astonishing growth and acceptance in developing economies. Two-thirds of the increase in power generation from renewable energies is happening in countries outside of the OECD, so these countries are expected to account for 62 percent of the total renewables generation by 2035, which is up from 53 percent in 2011 [12]. Almost one-third of the total growth in generation from renewables is because of China, which is more than the shares of the European Union, the United States, and Japan combined. Likewise, a significant growth of renewables is seen in Latin America, India, Africa, and Southeast Asia, driven mainly by regulations and incentives.

The solar energy industry is particularly growing fast, as it has attracted 12 billion U.S. dollars equivalent to 43 percent of the total clean energy investments from 2009 to 2013 [14]. After the solar, the wind industry attracted another 7.7 billion U.S. dollars investment between 2009 and 2013. Thus, solar and wind combined accounted for more than 70 percent of all investment in alternative energies. Biofuels and geothermal sectors attracted more than 2.2 billion U.S. dollars in investments [14]. As there is more interest in solar energy, the cost is declining fast. Solar photovoltaic is expected to become 40 to 70 percent more affordable in the next three decades. Wind is one of the fastest growing renewable technologies in power generation because it is cheaper than new natural gas plants. The modern wind power industry originated in Denmark, Germany, and the United States, but rapidly received acceptance in many parts of the world, including China that is becoming the industry leader in terms of installations [15]. In addition to Europe, China, and the United States, other developed and developing economies, notably Canada, Brazil, Mexico, South Africa, and India, have become important markets. Similar to the solar sector, falling prices and technology improvements are fueling the popularity of wind turbines, enabling the wind industry to compete with substitute sources, particularly with fossil fuels. In 2015, Denmark and Germany, respectively, generated 42 percent and 13 percent of their electricity from wind turbines [9]. As of 2014, more than 90 countries were relying on over 240,000 wind turbines to generate electricity [15].

The renewable energy sources will account for almost 60 percent of all new power generation capacity by 2040. It is estimated that, shortly before 2040, most of the renewables-based electricity generation will become economically competitive without any subsidies [2]. Currently, subsidies to renewable energies are estimated around 150 billion U.S. dollars, some 80 percent of which are directed to the power sector, 18 percent to transport, and around 1 percent to heat [2]. Innovative business models, new utility imperatives, and resilient electric grids are encouraging the adoption of distributed renewable generation. As the share of power generated by intermittent sources like wind and solar increases, technological advances are introducing the methods to ensure the power quality and reliability of electric grids [15].

Growing Demand for Natural Resources

Natural resources, including water, air, land, forests, fish and wildlife, topsoil, and minerals, are central to economic growth and to every aspect of life in our modern societies. About 50 percent of the global resource extraction is concentrated in Asia, followed by North America with almost 20 percent and Europe and Latin America with 13 percent each [16]. There are significant disparities in natural resources extraction per capita across the world. For instance, the natural resource extraction per capita in Australia is 10 times more than that in Asia or Africa. Currently, we consume 60 billion tons of natural resources each year or around 50 percent more than 30 years ago [17]. The extraction of natural resources could increase to 100 billion tons by 2030. While technological improvements, changing economic structures, and innovation have reduced the material intensity of the modern economy, an absolute surge in the demand for natural resources is inevitable [18]. Natural resources, particularly minerals, are increasingly used in higher quantities because of the rising world population, burgeoning industries, and new applications. Since the 18th century, the world population has increased exponentially from 1 billion in the 1830s to 2 billion in the 1930s, and 3 billion in the 1960s, and 7 billion in 2011. This rate of growth means that the global population has experienced an astonishing surge of 133 percent in 50 years between 1960 and 2011. The global population is projected to increase to 11 billion by 2100 (United Nations 2016). In addition to the global population growth, other factors such as rapid urbanization, economic development, and the spread of prosperity in developing or emerging economies such as Brazil, Russia, India, and China are poised to boost the consumption of natural resources in coming years [19]. For instance, China is urbanizing quickly and is expected to develop more than 200 cities with more than 1 million inhabitants by 2025 [25, 27]. As emerging countries attain economic development, a larger share of their populations becomes prosperous and naturally, increase their consumption of a variety of products and services, including cars, cell phones, and traveling. These changes in emerging countries have resulted in an unprecedented price explosion of many commodities in the past decade [29]. The financial crisis of 2007–2008 only temporarily brought down the prices of commodities and natural resources. The emerging economies still are at fueling the demand for natural resources. Furthermore, new technologies and industries not only use larger quantities of natural resources, but also require diverse metals and materials. In other words, at the global level, more material per unit of the GDP is now required. For example, a modern computer chip may use half of the elements in the Periodic Table [26]. In the past 20 years, the shortening products' lifecycles and proliferation of electronic devices such as smartphones and computers have aggravated the demand for natural resources even further.

The higher demand for natural resources moves exploration and extraction into new environments, requires new investments and technologies, and needs adequate regulatory frameworks [19]. The production of natural resources involves environmental damages such as the destruction of fertile land, water shortages, or toxic pollution. In addition to the physical damage, the extraction and production of natural resources may cause negative social consequences, including human rights violations, government corruption, poor working conditions, and low wages, particularly in African, Latin American, and Asian countries with low environmental and social standards [16].

International Trade of Natural Resources

In tandem with the growing demand and rising prices, international trade in materials and commodities continues to grow. International trade in natural resources is growing much faster than their extraction. For example, the international trade in materials has expanded fourfold since 1970. In 2010, more than 10 billion tons of material were traded internationally [27]. Natural resources are unequally distributed across the world, and their consumption often takes place far away from their extraction sites. Thus, international trade serves the redistribution of natural resources across the world and provides opportunities for both producers and consumers. In the past four decades, international trade in natural resources has become more specialized, particularly in fossil fuels and metal ores [27].

The international trade in natural resources is beneficial to both resource-rich and resource-poor countries. On the one hand, it allows the resource-rich countries to export resources and raises revenues. On the other hand, it supplies the resource-poor countries with their highly needed materials and commodities. Supposedly, the international trade in natural resources should bring about socio-economic development, cooperation, and prosperity. In practice, trade in resources often causes pernicious consequences, including corruption, environmental degradation, pollution, resource depletion, poverty, and conflict. The exporters of raw materials are mainly developing economies, while the importers include the industrialized countries of Europe and North America and the emerging countries such as China that export manufactured and high-added value products [16]. As the importers of natural resources are mainly industrialized and rich economies, they use the global trade of natural resources to increase resource consumption beyond their own national resource capacities [16]. Therefore, as international trade in natural resources increases, a growing number of countries become net importers of natural resources and increase their levels of consumption. Importing and exporting of countries are affected by resource price volatility, but in opposite directions [28]. The importing countries often benefit from low prices of materials while they are harmed by higher prices. By contrast, the exporting countries gain from higher prices and are badly hit by low prices of natural resources [27].

Price Volatility

In addition to reaching higher price levels, natural resources have been experiencing the patterns of significant price volatility in the past two decades since 2000 [18]. Prices for fuel, food, minerals, and metals have often fluctuated dramatically in recent years. According to the International Monetary Fund, fuel prices soared around 234 percent during 2003–2008, and mining products rose 178 percent during the same period [34]. The price volatility has become the new normal in the commodities markets. The high level of price volatility affects the revenues from resource producers, the output, and the investments. The resource-dependent economies that rely on a few commodities for the majority of their revenue may severely suffer from price volatility. On many occasions, the high levels of price fluctuations caused economic, social, and political instability. A sudden fall of the commodities prices may increase pressure on the sustenance of the poor populations in resource-dependent countries and lead to social tumult and conflict. For instance, in 2011, the high food and energy prices caused a doubling of inflation rates in many low-income countries where these items make up half of the consumer expenditure [21]. Furthermore, price volatility may discourage adequate investment in resources sectors, thus causing resource shortages as happened in 2008. Price volatility increases risk margins, and as a result, impedes investment in production and supply. Furthermore, short-term and frequent price variations may reduce the supply and cause disruptions that cause higher prices in long term [20]. Increasingly, consumers, producers, manufacturers, and retailers are susceptible to destabilizing effects of short-term price volatility [18].

Global Perils of Water Scarcity

Water covers almost 70 percent of the planet, but only 2.5 percent of all water is suitable for human needs. Currently, some 1.2 billion people or 20 percent of the world's population live in areas marked by water scarcity, and another 1.6 billion people face some degree of water shortage [22]. According to the United Nations reports, as early as 2000, approximately one billion people lacked access to safe drinking water and almost 2.5 billion required acceptable sanitation [23]. It is estimated that, currently, 1.8 billion people or almost 25 percent of the global population uses a source of drinking water contaminated by feces [24]. The rising water demand and lack of access to safe drinking water result in five million deaths each year due to water-related illness. The problem will only worsen as the global growth in water demand is expected to increase by 50 percent over the next two decades. The fast and extraordinary growth in water demand will overtake the ability of many ecosystems and human management to supply clean water [35]. By 2025, four billion people will be living in conditions of water stress and another 1.8 billion people will be living in regions with absolute water scarcity [30, 31].

Population growth, climate change, urbanization, agriculture, industrialization, changes in diets and lifestyle, investment and management shortfalls, and inefficient use of existing resources are among the main causes of water scarcity. Water consumption increases at approximately twice the rate of population growth, as more fresh water is required not only for basic drinking needs, but for food production, industry, and improving human health [32]. Globally, 70 percent of water withdrawals are for the agricultural sector, 11 percent for municipal demands, and 19 percent for industrial needs [38]. According to the United Nations Population Division, the world population has more than doubled since the 1950s and is expected to exceed eight billion in 2024, 9 billion in 2038, and 10 billion in 2056. These levels of population growth will put huge pressure on water resources to meet increased food, energy, and industrial demands [33]. Ironically, food and agriculture are the most water-intensive sectors and account for more than 90 percent of water use [40]. The importance of water resources for food and agriculture is rising, as the world is adding more inhabitants and as developing economies are becoming wealthier and their citizens are shifting from starch-based diets to meat and dairy, which require more water. For instance, producing 1 kilogram of rice requires about 3,500 liters of water, while producing 1 kilogram of beef needs some 15,000 liters [36]. Likewise, water scarcity will be aggravated by energy sector, as all forms of energy require water at the production, conversion, distribution, and consumption stages.

Water scarcity has a broad meaning and can refer to physical scarcity or economic scarcity of water. Physical water scarcity implies that there is not enough water to meet demand. Economic water scarcity means an absence of investment and proper management to meet the demand of consumers to use existing water sources [37]. There are many methods to measure water scarcity. For instance, we can compare the size of a population with the amount of available water. According to the United Nations guidelines, water stress for a region happens when the annual water supplies fall below 1,700 cubic meters per person and water scarcity for a region happens when water supplies are less than 1,000 cubic meters per person [39]. Middle East, North Africa, Caucasus, and Central Asia, Mongolia, Pakistan, India, Afghanistan, Horn of Africa, and South Sudan are on the top of the list of water-stressed regions (see Figures 1.3 and 1.4). What is more, all these regions suffer from high economic inequality and weak governance. The Asia-Pacific region contains

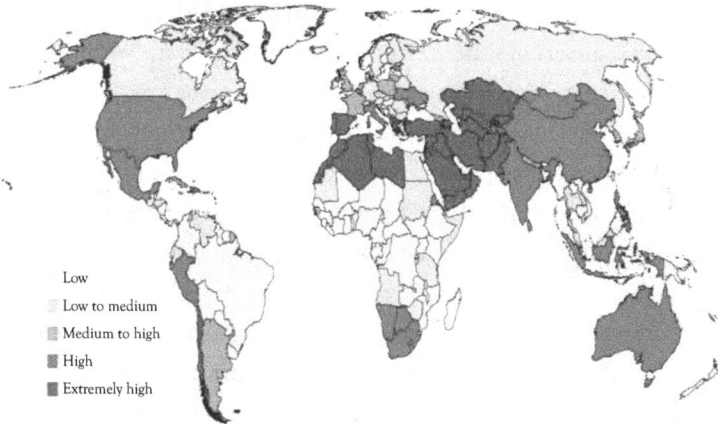

Low

Low to medium

Medium to high

High

Extremely high

Figure 1.3 Country-level water stress in 2040 under the business-as-usual scenario

Source: [42].

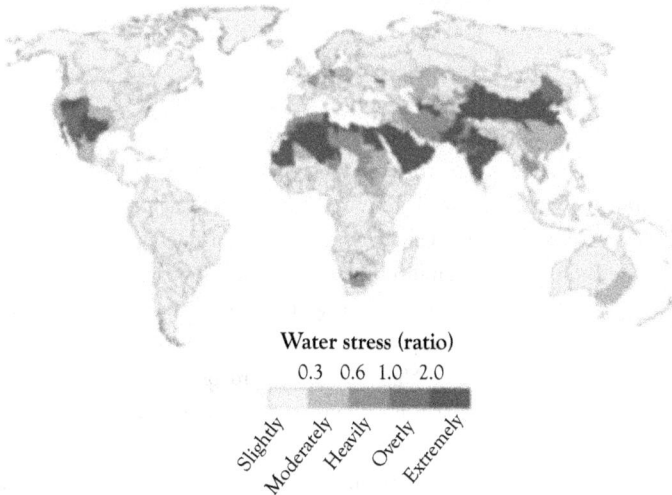

Water stress (ratio)

0.3 0.6 1.0 2.0

Slightly Moderately Heavily Overly Extremely

Figure 1.4 Water stress, shown in the global distribution of water stress index (WSI)

Source: [31].

over 50 percent of the world's population, but detains only 36 percent of the global water resources. All Arab countries are considered water-scarce, with less than 500 cubic meters of renewable water resources available per person [40]. Similarly, more than 66 percent of Africa is arid or semi-arid, and more than 300 million people in sub-Saharan Africa live on less than 1,000 cubic meters of water resources each. By contrast, North America and Europe enjoy high levels of renewable water resources. For example, Canada and the United States have about 85,310 and 9,888 cubic meters of water resources per person, respectively, whereas Europe has almost 4,741 cubic meters [41]. Apart from its biological and economic importance, water is becoming a hot global and geopolitical issue in some regions. Water insecurity can be aggravated by drought. As water availability decreases, competition for access to this vital, but limited resource will increase. Around 60 percent of all freshwater comes from internationally shared river basins that could become sources of cross-national competition [24]. Water scarcity could involve serious socio-economic risks across the world, including famines and food shortages, migratory pressures, regional destabilization, economic downturn, increasing dependence on foreign aid, and diplomatic and national conflict over trans-boundary water resources.

References

[1] Conti, J., P. Holtberg, J. Diefenderfer, A. LaRose, J.T. Turnure, and L. Westfall. 2016. *International Energy Outlook 2016 With Projections to 2040 (No. DOE/EIA-0484)*. USDOE Energy Information Administration (EIA). Washington, DC (United States). Office of Energy Analysis.

[2] Energy Information Administration (US), and Government Publications Office, eds. 2016. *International Energy Outlook 2016: With Projections to 2040*. Government Printing Office.

[3] Hoffman, L.A., and T.T. Ngo. 2018. "Affordable Solar Thermal Water Heating Solution for the Rural Dominican Republic." *Renewable Energy* 115, pp. 1220–30.

[4] OCHA Occasional Policy Briefing Series. 2010. "Brief No. 3: Energy Security and Humanitarian Action: Key Emerging Trends and Challenges." Available at https://unocha.org/sites/unocha/files/Energy%20Security%20 and%20Humanitarian%20Action.pdf

[5] Mobil, E. 2015. "The Outlook of Energy: A View to 2040." https://cdn. exxonmobil.com/~/media/global/files/outlook-for-energy/2016/2016-outlook-for-energy.pdf

[6] Atlantic Review. 2013. https://theatlantic.com/technology/archive/2013/12/ heres-why-developing-countries-will-consume-65-of-the-worlds-energy-by-2040/282006/

[7] Global Trends in Oil and Gas Markets to 2025. 2013. *Lukoil,* https://lukoil. be/pdf/Trends_Global_Oil_ENG.pdf

[8] ANNEX, WEB. 2013. "Global Trends and Future Challenges for the Work of the Organization." Available at: http://fao.org/3/a-au903e.pdf

[9] World Energy Resources, 2016. World Energy Council, https://worldenergy. org/publications/2016/world-energy-resources-2016/

[10] Pound, W. 2010. *Meeting the Energy Challenges of the Future a Guide for Policymakers.*

[11] The Oil and Gas Industry. 2015. *Overview and Trends. NRGI Reader,* April 2015. Available at https://resourcegovernance.org/sites/default/files/nrgi_ Oil-and-Gas-Industry.pdf

[12] Outlook, S.A.E. 2013. *World Energy Outlook Special Report.* France International Energy Agency (IEA).

[13] Statistisches Bundesamt. 2017. "Bruttostromerzeugung 2013." Available on https://destatis.de/DE/ZahlenFakten/ImFokus/Energie/ErneuerbareEnergien 2013.html (accessed July 10, 2017).

[14] Power Shifts Emerging Clean Energy Markets. May 2015. "A Report from the Pew Charitable Trusts." http://pewtrusts.org/~/media/assets/2015/05/ emerging-markets-report_web.pdf

[15] Lins, C., L.E. Williamson, S. Leitner, and S. Teske. 2014. "The First Decade: 2004–2014: 10 Years of Renewable Energy Progress." *Renewable Energy Policy Network for the 21st Century.*

[16] Giljum, S., F. Hinterberger, M. Bruckner, E. Burger, J. Frühmann, S. Lutter, and M. Warhurst. 2009. *Overconsumption? Our Use of the World's Natural Resources.*

[17] Dadush, U.B., and S. Ali. 2012. *In Search of the Global Middle Class: A New Index.* Carnegie Endowment for International Peace.

[18] Natural Resources in 2020, 2030, and 2040: Implications for the United States.

[19] Lusty, P.A.J., and A.G. Gunn. 2014. "Challenges to Global Mineral Resource Security and Options for Future Supply." *Geological Society.* London, Special Publications, 393, SP393–12.

[20] Lee, B., F. Preston, J. Kooroshy, R. Bailey, and G. Lahn. 2012. *Resources Futures,* 14 vols. London: Chatham House.

[21] IMF 2011. "Managing Global Growth Risks and Commodity Price Shocks: Vulnerabilities and Policy Challenges for Low-Income Countries." *International Monetary Fund,* http://imf.org/external/np/pp/ eng/2011/092111.pdf

[22] UN-Water. 2013. "Water for Life 2005-2015: Water Scarcity." at www.un.org/waterforlifedecade/scarcity.shtml (accessed February 20, 2013).

[23] Padowski, J.C., and J.W. Jawitz. 2009. "The Future of Global Water Scarcity: Policy and Management Challenges and Opportunities." *Whitehead J. Dipl. & Int'l Rel.* 10, p. 99.

[24] Metcalfe, C., L. Guppy, and M. Qadir. 2017. *Global Barriers To Improving Water Quality: A Critical Review*. United Nations University Institute for Water, Environment, and Health.

[25] Woetzel, J., L. Mendonca, J. Devan, S. Negri, Y. Hu, L. Jordan, and F. Yu. 2009. *Preparing for China's Urban Billion*. McKinsey Global Institute Report.

[26] Graedel, T.E., E.M. Harper, T. Nassar, and B.K. Reck. 2013. "On the Materials Basis of Modern Society." *Proceedings of the National Academy of Sciences*. First Published Online December 2, 2013, http://dx.doi.org/10.1073/pnas.1312752110

[27] Schandl, H., M. Fischer-Kowalski, J. West, S. Giljum, M. Dittrich, N. Eisenmenger, and F. Krausmann. 2017. "Global Material Flows and Resource Productivity." *Assessment Report for the UNEP International Resource Panel*. Pre-publication Final Draft.

[28] Trends to Watch in Alternative Energy. 2016. Deloitte US, https://www2.deloitte.com/us/en/pages/energy-and-resources/articles/alternative-energy-trends.html

[29] De Ridder, M. 2013. *The Geopolitics of Mineral Resources for Renewable Energy Technologies*. The Hague Centre for Strategic Studies.

[30] World Water Assessment Programme (WWAP). 2012. *World Water Development Report*, Vol. 1: *Managing Water Under Uncertainty and Risk*. Paris: UNESCO.

[31] Schlosser, C.A., K. Strzepek, X. Gao, C. Fant, E. Blanc, S. Paltsev, and A. Gueneau. 2014. "The Future of Global Water Stress: An Integrated Assessment." *Earth's Future* 2, no. 8, pp. 341–61.

[32] UN-Water. 2006. *Coping with Water Scarcity-A Strategic Issue and Priority for System-wide Action*. UN-Water Thematic Initiatives.

[33] UN-Water. 2013. "Statistics: Graphs & Maps." Available at www.unwater.org/statistics_use.html (accessed February 22, 2013).

[34] Kumar, S. 2013. "The Looming Threat of Water Scarcity." *In Vital Signs*, 96–100. Washington, DC: Island Press.

[35] Padowski, J.C., and J.W. Jawitz. 2009. "The Future of Global Water Scarcity: Policy and Management Challenges and Opportunities." *Whitehead J. Dipl. and Int'l Rel.* 10, p. 99.

[36] FAO, AQUASTAT. 2013. Available at fao.org/nr/water/aquastat/water_use/index.stm (accessed March 1, 2013).

[37] U.N. Food and Agriculture Organization (FAO). 2012. *Coping with Water Scarcity: An Action Framework for Agriculture and Food Security*. FAO Water Report 38 Rome.

[38] FAO, AQUASTAT, at www.fao.org/nr/water/aquastat/water_use/index. stm, viewed 1 March 2013

[39] World Water Assessment Programme (WWAP). 2012. *World Water Development Report, Vol. 1: Managing Water Under Uncertainty and Risk.* Paris: UNESCO.

[40] Water under Uncertainty and Risk. 2012. Paris: UNESCO.

[41] Worldwatch Calculation Based on Total Renewable Water Resources from FAO, op. cit. note 12; Total Renewable Water Resources from European Environment Agency, "Water Availability," at www.eea.europa.eu/themes/ water/water-resources/water-availability, February 18, 2008; population data from U.N. Department of Economic and Social Affairs, at esa.un.org/ unpd/wpp/Excel-Data/population.htm (accessed March 1, 2013).

[42] Luo, T., R. Young, and P. Reig. 2015. *Aqueduct Projected Water Stress Country Rankings*. Technical Note.

CHAPTER 2

Food and Agriculture

Global Patterns of Hunger and Undernourishment

The current trends portray a mixed and complex picture of global hunger and undernourishment. Despite a rapidly growing global population, the share of undernourished people has decreased across the planet over the course of the past decades. For instance, the world population has increased by 1.9 billion between 1992 and 2016, but the share of undernourished people has dropped from 18.6 percent to 10.9 percent [1]. The number of undernourished people has decreased almost by 216 million for the same period [1]. Most of the improvement in fighting malnutrition and reducing hunger was achieved before the 1990s, but since the early 2000s, the rate of improvement in undernourishment has slowed, and in some regions, has reversed. In the past two decades, the main progress in fighting undernourishment has been concentrated in populous regions such as China, Southeast Asia, and South America [3]. Since the 2000s, the absolute number of people wrecked by hunger continues to grow [2]. According to the Food and Agriculture Organization (FAO) of the United Nations, global hunger is on the rise again, affecting 815 million in 2016 or 11 percent of the global population.

The distribution of hunger varies significantly across the world. In 2010, almost 30 percent of the population in sub-Saharan Africa was undernourished, while the largest number of undernourished people (600 million) lived in Asia [2] (see Figures 2.1 and 2.2). The global distribution of hunger is so skewed that two-thirds of the world's undernourished people live in seven countries, namely, Bangladesh, China, the Democratic Republic of Congo, Ethiopia, India, Indonesia, and

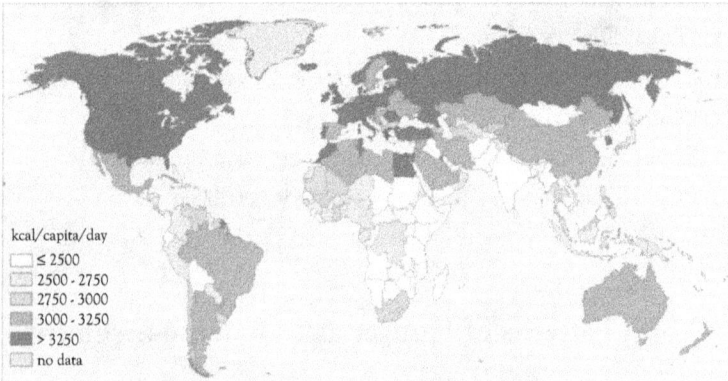

Figure 2.1 *World food availability per capita (average 2009–2011)*

Source: [5].

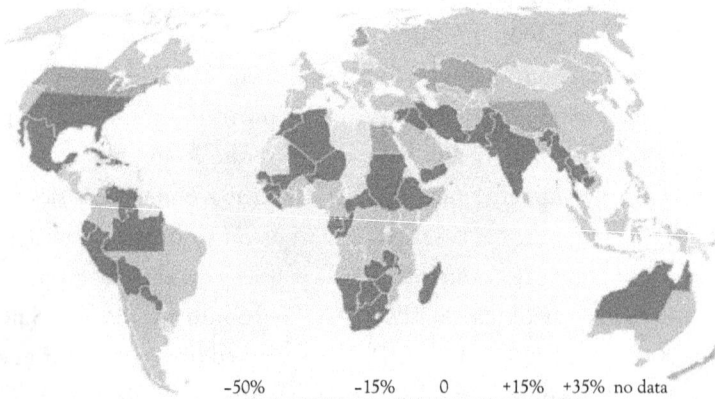

Figure 2.2 *Projected changes in agriculture in 2080 due to climate change*

Source: [5].

Pakistan [4]. According to the United Nations, the world's population will grow by almost two billion people in the next three decades, and most of this growth will happen in sub-Saharan Africa and India. What makes the fight against hunger more difficult is the fact that most of the global population growth happens in extremely poor and undernourished regions. As rural populations grow much faster than employment and productivity in primary agriculture, the undernourishment in rural areas is more prevalent than in urban centers [3]. To reduce the associated undernourishment, governments and policy-makers in developing economies should enable the transition of their economies to non-agricultural employment. However, this transition requires some significant instructional and societal reforms. In Asia and Latin America, a large proportion of the rural population is moving to non-agricultural jobs, but in sub-Saharan Africa, the share of rural labor employed in non-agricultural jobs is still negligible [5]. Some countries and regions, including the Caucasus and Central Asia, Eastern Asia, Latin America, and Northern Africa, have shown astonishing progress in reducing undernourishment. By contrast, Southern Asia and sub-Saharan Africa have shown little improvement in the fight against undernourishment and hunger. Therefore, Southern Asia and sub-Saharan Africa account for significantly higher shares of undernourishment in the world. The food security and undernourishment have deteriorated in many parts of sub-Saharan Africa, South Eastern, and Western Asia due to a wide range of factors, including violent conflicts, political turmoil, water scarcity, droughts, and climate change. Recurrent extreme climate conditions and natural disasters increasingly cause economic damage and reduce agricultural productivity.

There is a vicious and reciprocal relationship between violent conflicts and the prevalence of undernourishment or hunger. Indeed, more than 60 percent of food-insecure and undernourished people in the world live in the countries affected by violent conflict. Most of the world's conflicts are concentrated in four regions: the Near East and North Africa, sub-Saharan Africa, Central America, and Eastern Europe. Violent conflicts disturb almost every aspect of agricultural activities and food systems from production, harvesting, processing, and transport to financing and marketing [1]. The causal relationship between undernourishment and conflict seems reciprocal. In other words, undernourishment can be considered as both the cause and consequence of conflict. It is widely recognized that food shortage is among the main causes of conflict. For example, the socio-political turmoil in many Arab countries in 2011, known in the media as the Arab Spring, could be attributed to food insecurity and significant surges in the food prices between 2009 and 2010. Likewise, violent conflicts and social turmoil in the Horn of Africa and Eastern Africa have been linked to lingering famine and food shortages.

In addition to acute undernourishment, a large number of people or almost one in three people worldwide are suffering from chronic malnutrition [6]. It is estimated that more than two billion people do not have access to vital micronutrients. The forms of malnutrition are diverse and are expected to involve serious risks. For instance, a growing number of the world population is suffering from the pernicious effects of obesity and diet-related diseases such as diabetes and hypertension. The occurrence of obesity more than doubled between in the last three decades between 1980 and 2014 [1]. More than 600 million adults, almost 13 percent of the world's adult population, are categorized as obese. In Latin America, almost 25 percent of the adult population is currently obese. The share of overweight people is rising in every region and most rapidly in low- and middle-income countries [6]. For example, the number of overweight adults in China is projected to increase 50 percent by 2030.

Growing Demand for Food

The global demand for food is expected to grow in the next three decades, driven by a significant surge in the world population compounded by economic growth and increases in consumption per capita across the globe, and particularly, in developing economies. While the world population growth has slowed since the mid-1980s, it remains at about 1.2 percent per year. Currently, the world population is estimated at 7.5 billion, and according to the United Nations Population Division, it is expected to increase to 9.8 billion by 2050 and 11.2 billion by 2100 [31]. Food consumption follows and often surpasses population growth, especially in the developing economies marked by improvement in the income per capita. The drivers for an improved income per capita include productivity gains, industrialization, better education, government spending on infrastructure, and higher levels of consumption [7]. Food consumption per capita has grown in the past 50 years from an average of 2,280 kcal/person/day in the early 1960s to almost 2,800 kcal/person/day in 2014. The Western industrialized countries reached high levels of food consumption per capita as early as the 1960s, but most of the gains in recent years are attributed to the developing and emerging economies [3].

Each year, the world population increases by more than 100 million of which the majority is in developing economies of Asia and Africa. Africa has the highest growth rate at 2.5 percent, while Europe has the lowest growth rate of 0.04 percent. As a result, most of the global population growth in the next four decades is expected to happen in Africa. Other developing economies, including India, Egypt, and Pakistan, will witness substantial population growth at least until 2050. By contrast, population growth in most developed economies is small or even negative. The significant divergence between the population growth in the rich or developed and the poor or developing economies implies that most of the future demand for food will originate from the latter, not the former. This implies that the demand for all major agricultural commodity groups will continue to grow.

It is hard to predict the future demand for food, but some estimates reveal that the demand for food may increase as much as 70 percent by 2050 [8]. In order to meet the demand in 2050, food production in developing economies should double. For example, the annual cereal production would have to grow by almost one billion tons and meat production by over 200 million tons to a total of 470 million tons in 2050 [8]. Because of the projected economic growth in developing economies, the demand for food products such as livestock and dairy products that are more responsive to higher incomes is expected to grow much faster than that for cereals.

In the past 10 years, production growth is accelerating for some commodities, such as oilseeds, cereals, and milk, while it is slowing down for other, such as eggs and meat [7]. Overall, we can say that the demand for all major agricultural commodities in the developed regions has reached a state of maturity or is growing at a moderate pace, but the demand in the developing regions of the world marked by high population growth is still growing fast. Therefore, the demand for most agricultural products,

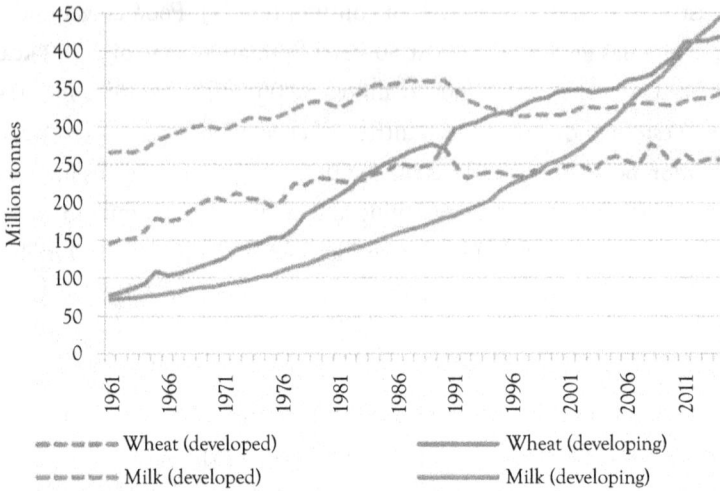

Figure 2.3 Evolution of consumption of wheat and milk in the developed and developing economies

Source: [4].

including milk, beef, and poultry, from developing economies is surpassing the demand from developed economies [7] (see Figures 2.3 and 2.4). The food consumption growth is expected to outpace the population growth for the major commodity groups, mainly due to the increasing income levels. The only exceptions could be meat and dairy products that their consumption levels seem either stable or decreasing. The beef consumption growth rate has dropped below the population growth rate due to a declining consumption in developed economies and rising prices that reduce the products' affordability.

Global Dietary Changes

In recent years, a multitude of factors, including economic development, urbanization, higher income levels, international trade, and cultural adaptation, have contributed to a dietary transformation across the world. Diets have moved away from staples such as cereals, roots, and tubers toward more livestock products, meat, milk, vegetable oils, fruits, and vegetables, in both developing and developed nations [3]. Consumers are adding diverse and more expensive foodstuffs to their diets.

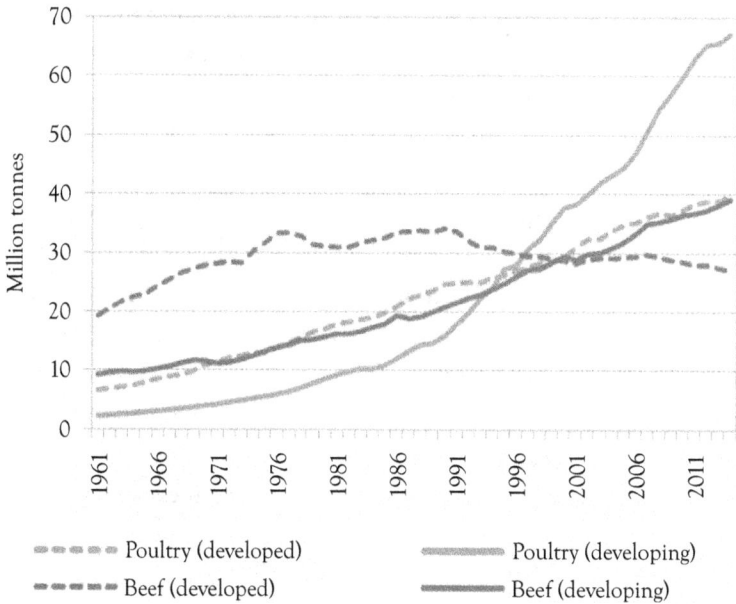

Figure 2.4 Evolution of consumption of poultry and beef in the developed and developing economies

Source: [4].

In developed economies, consumers often can afford their preferred foods, and the effects of income increase and economic growth on their diet are generally negligible. By contrast, in developing economies, economic growth and increases in income levels are drastically changing the dietary habits. In these countries, as wages increase, consumers are more likely to pay for packaged, prepared, and processed foods.

In addition to economic development, urbanization may have important effects on consumers' dietary preferences. For the first time in 2007, the world's urban population has surpassed the world's rural population. According to the World Bank reports, the share of the world's urban population has risen from 30 percent in 1950 to more than 54 percent in 2015. Rural residents often consume traditional foods that are high in grains, fruit and vegetables, and low in fat; by contrast, urban residents tend to consume an increased intake of energy, sugar, refined grains, and fats [9]. As urban centers attract large supermarket chains, they make non-traditional foods more accessible to urban populations

[10]. Furthermore, urban consumers generally spend less time at home, enjoy higher income levels, have smaller households, and conduct a busy lifestyle. Therefore, urban consumers are more likely to consume processed or fast food. In urban centers, foodstuffs such as bread, noodles, pizza, and pasta are popular, and meat, fruits, and vegetables are preferred [11]. It is widely accepted that urbanization stimulates the global demand for animal proteins, fat, salt, sugar, and refined carbohydrates, and discourages the demand for fiber and micronutrient [12]. In addition to urbanization, international business, advertising, and telecommunication are pushing people from developing countries to adopt the North American and European dietary habits [13]. Consequently, the patterns of food consumption are becoming more similar across the world.

At the global level, there has been an increasing pressure on the livestock sector to meet the growing demand for animal protein [14]. Calorie and protein intakes have remained stable in developed economies, while they have been growing sharply in developing economies [7]. Meat consumption in developing economies has grown from 10 kilograms per person per year in 1964–1966 to 26 in 1997–1999 and may reach 37 kilograms per person per year in 2030 [15]. Likewise, the consumption of milk and dairy products in developing economies has risen from 28 kilograms per person per year in 1964–1966 to 45 kilograms in 1997–1999 and is poised to reach 66 kilograms by 2030 [13]. In developing economies, cereals, rice, vegetable oil, sugar, meat, and dairy intake are consumed higher than the last three decades, and the consumption of all animal products, including meat, dairy, fish, and eggs, is growing very fast [7]. There is a strong positive relationship between the level of income and consumption of animal protein [16]. Therefore, as the income levels across the world and particularly in emerging countries increase, there will be more demand for the animal sources of protein, including meat, chicken, fish, milk, and eggs. The increasing interest in meat and animal-derived foods may lead to food shortage. Furthermore, meat production generates more greenhouse gas emissions and causes other environmental damages such as deforestation, farmland degradation, and depletion of water resources [17].

The dietary changes and increasing food consumption per capita, combined with a more sedentary lifestyle, have led to the prevalence of obesity and a number of diet-related and non-communicable diseases such as type 2 diabetes and heart diseases in developing economies [18, 19, 20]. It is increasingly common to see obesity and malnutrition or undernourishment next to each other in developing economies [21]. According to the World Health Organization, in 2014, more than 1.9 billion adults or more than 25 percent of the world's population was overweight. Almost, two-third of the overweight people now live in developing countries, particularly in emerging markets and transition economies. Indeed, due to the recent changes in their diets, many developing economies are facing the double burden of malnutrition and obesity at the same time.

Rising Productivity Gaps Between the Developed and Developing Economies

Throughout the 20th century, agricultural productivity has largely increased across the world, and therefore, the food production growth has matched or surpassed the population growth. According to the United Nation FAO, almost 70 percent of the improvement in agricultural productivity is attributable to increasing yields, while the expansion of arable land and increase of the cropping frequency has limited effects on the overall agricultural improved productivity. The noticeable development is that agricultural yields have increased mainly in industrial countries and China. Indeed, developing economies, particularly the Sub-Saharan African countries, have shown no or very limited levels of yield improvement [13] (see Figure 2.5). In the past decades, the advent of new technologies has modernized agricultural production in the developed economies of Western Europe, Oceania, and North America. New technologies have delivered the means for motorization and large-scale mechanization, mineral fertilization, treatment of pests, diseases, and conservation and processing of vegetable and animal products in developed economies [13]. As new machines were used in agriculture, smaller farms were consolidated into larger ones, and the share of farmers' population declined substantially [23]. For example, the number of farms in the United States fell from about six million in 1950 to about two million in 2000 [22]. The agricultural sector has continued to become more effective by producing more crops with fewer workers and resources. According to the

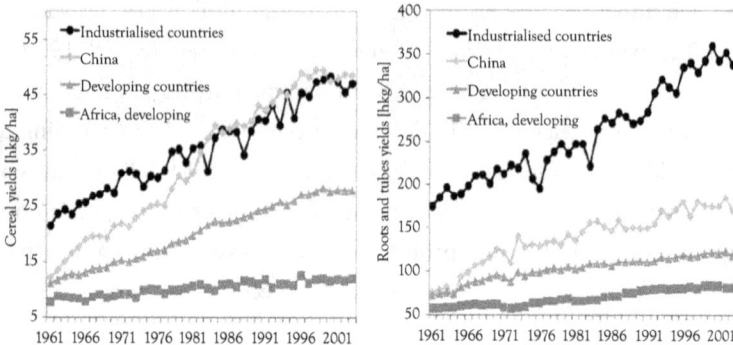

Figure 2.5 *Yields of cereals plus roots and tubes in industrialized and developing economies plus in China and Africa, developing from 1961 to 2003*

Source: [2].

U.S. Department of Agriculture [19], in 2015, direct on-farm employment accounted only for about 2.6 million jobs or 1.4 percent of the U.S. employment. The agricultural modernization resulted in higher efficiency, thus higher volumes and lower prices of agricultural produces that became competitive in international markets. The transformation of agricultural production in industrialized countries not only liberated a significant share of workers from agricultural production, but also provided abundant and cheap food that allowed consumers to spend only a small percentage of their income on food. In 2016, food accounted for almost 12.6 percent of the American households' expenditures [19]. In addition, the consumers in the United States and other developed economies got access to a larger variety of food products from meat, chicken, and fish to fresh fruits and vegetables, independent of season or their geographical location.

The modernization of agricultural production in developing economies has seen significant setbacks. In most developing countries, farms' sizes are usually small, the use of farm planning is not well established, and farming techniques have remained mainly simple and inefficient. Farmers in developing countries generally cannot afford the new agricultural equipment. Because in developing countries, a largely rural population of landless households relies on agricultural production, the arrival of agricultural machines and adoption of new techniques could involve adverse effects on farmers. With the rising competition in international markets, farmers in developing countries have to adopt modern agricultural practices, including the increased use of chemical fertilizers and pesticides. Due to the mounting competitive and international pressures, the farmers in developing countries are forced to concentrate on short-term returns from cash crops [23]. As the farmers emphasize cash crops, local food production declines and the developing countries become more dependent on food imports from industrialized countries [23]. In the early 1960s, developing countries were considered as food exporters and had a general agricultural trade surplus of almost seven billion U.S. dollars per year. However, since the 1980s, the net flow of agricultural commodities between developed and developing countries has reversed direction, and most developing countries have become net importers of agricultural products [3]. The improvement in agricultural productivity and falling real prices of agricultural products are certainly beneficial to world consumers and may increase the economic status of the urban poor in developing countries. However, the abundance of food products due to increased price competition may harm developing countries whose populations traditionally remain dependent on agricultural production to survive [13].

Emerging Techniques in Agriculture and Food Production

The food production is being reshaped by certain emerging technologies in areas such as biology, materials science, seasonal forecasting, and computer science. Agricultural biotechnologies range from low-tech approaches, including artificial insemination, fermentation techniques, and bio-fertilizers, to high-tech approaches and advanced DNA-based methods like genetically modified organisms [30]. The emerging techniques in biological science will deliver crops, pastures, and animals, which could provide higher-value products, including cereals with enhanced health attributes, novel aquaculture breeds and feeds, and designed plants with bio-industrial applications. Modern genetics can improve agricultural productivity, natural resource management, and consumer demand. The emerging genomic techniques can be used to develop more effective farming methods for the dry tropics, shifting crop and animal production systems into new climatic zones, and improved resource-use efficiency across all agricultural systems. The advances in biotechnology may result in the creation of new types of animals and plants that can more effectively supply nutrients. Many new food products may be created directly from genetic manipulation or laboratory processes. Currently, it is possible to produce *in vitro* meat or the meat cultured directly in a lab. While no cultured meat has been produced for public consumption yet, this product is likely to gain economic justification and consumers' acceptance in the future.

Along with biotechnology, the advances in materials science offer custom design of special ingredients and supplies for agricultural applications, including fertilizer formulations, seed coatings, and germination control. Nanotechnology-based food and health products will be gradually available to consumers worldwide in the coming years [30]. Nanotechnology could not only increase soil fertility, but also develop innovative products and applications for agriculture, water treatment, food production, processing, preservation, and packaging [24]. Nanotechnology may be used to control how food looks, tastes, and even how long it lasts. The new information technology could lead to significant improvements in farming automation. In future, the digital farming platforms will allow farmers to use a wide range of robotics, including automated aerial and ground vehicles, drones, and associated intelligent software and data analytics for crops, automated milking, herding and sampling, and animal production systems. Consequently, farmers can boost their productivity, save on the cost of labor, and plan for their operations. The digital technologies such as computational decision and analytics tools, the cloud, sensors, and robots enable farmers to effectively utilize their data and optimize their production [25]. Agriculture will greatly benefit from increases in a better understanding of climate, improvements in observations, modeling techniques, and computer speed that will make seasonal forecasting more accurate. Farmers may rely on satellite imagery and advanced sensors to optimize returns on inputs. Crop imagery may help farmers scan crops as if they are present on the ground. By integrating sensors with satellite imagery, farmers can manage crop, soil, and water more effectively and conveniently. Technologies like global positioning systems (GPS), geographical information systems, precision soil sampling, proximal and remote spectroscopic sensing, robots, unmanned aerial vehicles, and auto-steered and guided equipment can help farmers substantially increase their productivity [25]. Agricultural robots may be used to automate agricultural processes, such as harvesting, fruit picking, plowing, soil maintenance, weeding, planting, and irrigation. Soil and water sensors can identify moisture and nitrogen levels, so farmers can use this information to determine when to water and fertilize their lands. Some new irrigation technologies can improve crop yields by 30 percent over crops grown without irrigation. Because most developing economies are still relying on traditional irrigation approaches, advanced irrigation technologies may result in significant increases in the agricultural output across the world [17]. The use of protected and greenhouse cultivation is a growing trend in agricultural production that can improve both the quality and quantity of crops. Currently, Spain, the Netherlands, and Israel are the leaders in protected and greenhouse cultivation [24]. Vertical farming could allow farmers to produce food in vertically stacked layers for instance in dense areas or within urban environments. All these technological advances will usher farmers into a new digital agriculture very like manufacturing and service sectors. Thus, a nation's agricultural productivity will depend even more on its technological competitiveness and innovation capacity.

Limited Arable Land and Application of Fertilizers

The total world's land area is estimated about 130.7 million km², of which only less than half is arable [26]. The bad news is that almost all of the world's arable land has been already exploited, and significant increases in arable land are practically impossible. A further expansion of arable land may include forests and grasslands, or those lands that are either too steep, too dry, or too wet. For instance, about 80 percent of deforestation in the past decades has been attributed to developing arable lands [26]. Obviously, deforestation is not a viable solution as it causes many environmental problems, including loss of biodiversity and emission of greenhouse gases. While the expansion of arable land is not feasible, the existing agricultural land areas are gradually becoming less productive due to soil erosion, salinization, waterlog-ging, urbanization, nutrient depletion, over-cultivation, overgrazing, and soil compaction. Soil erosion is the most serious cause of arable land degradation that is associated with agricultural malpractices leav-ing the soil surface without vegetative cover for an extended period of time and exposing it to the effects of wind and rain [13]. Due to its noxious effects, land degradation should be considered a major threat to food security [27].

In the past few decades, the widespread application of nitrogen-based fertilizers has resulted in securing more agricultural products for the world's growing population, but at the same time, has caused an accu-mulation of huge amounts of reactive nitrogen in the soil and natural environment. Increases in reactive nitrogen in the atmosphere are linked to the production of tropospheric ozone and aerosols that affect human health and cause respiratory diseases, cancer, and cardiac diseases. Fur-thermore, the increased levels of reactive nitrogen may bring about water acidification, biodiversity losses in lakes, habitat degradation in coastal ecosystems, global climate change, and stratospheric ozone depletion [13, 28]. In addition to nitrogen-based fertilizers, agricultural pesticides involve serious toxic effects on the environment. For example, agricul-tural pesticides may enter surface and groundwater and may be toxic to aquatic organisms, as well as to terrestrial flora and fauna [29]. While the use of pesticides and fertilizers may be harmful to humans and the environment, in many developing regions of the world like Africa, India, and Central America, these chemicals are still under-used. Therefore, we can predict that, at the global level, the use of fertilizers such as nitrogen, phosphate, and potash along with their perverse effects will continue to increase in the near future.

Consolidation of Food Production and Distribution Systems

In recent years, the agricultural industry has undergone significant transformations, including the standardization of output, concen-tration of primary production, and consolidation of farmland [30]. Small landowners have left their farmlands in search of employment and opportunities in large cities. At the same time, food production is changing along with retail channels, and thus, value chains are becoming vertical, marked by the integration of primary production, processing, and distribution. Due to their limitations in financing, market accessibility, transport, and quality, many small and medium-sized businesses are giving up, and they cannot compete with big players anymore. Food producers are increasingly relying on automation, large-scale processing, and higher levels of capital to boost their output [30]. Because of these trends, the share of fresh food has been declining across the world. For instance, the share of fresh food has remained below 30 percent in upper-middle-income countries, and around 10 percent in lower-middle-income countries [30]. In many developed and developing economies, a large number of urbanized consumers are relying on a few supermarket chains to purchase their groceries. The food industry is particularly consolidated in North America where hypermarkets account for more than 93 percent of the food purchase. This pattern is quickly spreading to other parts of the world. The shares of hypermarkets in food distribution in Europe, Latin America, Middle East, and Africa and Asia are estimated respectively at 55, 46, 38, and 36 percent [30]. The consolidated and large-scale food producers could help increase the convenience and efficiency of food delivery systems. At the same time, they are likely to introduce processed food products that contain higher levels of sugar, fat, and salt. The share of processed food rose between 2000 and 2014 across the world in low-, middle-, and high-income countries. The significant rise in overweight, obesity, and diet-related non-communicable diseases across the world confirms the adverse effects of large-scale food producers and distributors on consumers' health.

References

[1]   Marx, A. 2015. *The State of Food Insecurity in the World: Meeting the 2015 International Hunger Targets: Taking Stock of Uneven Progress*. Rome: Food and Agriculture Organization of the United Nations.

[2]   Giovannucci, D., S.J. Scherr, D. Nierenberg, C. Hebebrand, J. Shapiro, J. Milder, and K. Wheeler. 2012. *Food and Agriculture: The Future of Sustainability*.

[3]   Wik, M., P. Pingali, and S. Brocai. 2008. *Global Agricultural Performance: Past Trends and Future Prospects.*

[4]   FAO, September 14, 2010. http://fao.org/news/story/en/item/45210/icode/

[5]   FAO, U. December, 2009. *How to Feed the World in 2050.* In Rome: High-Level Expert Forum.

[6]   Vasileska, A., and G. Rechkoska. 2012. "Global and Regional Food Consumption Patterns and Trends." *Procedia-Social and Behavioral Sciences* 44, pp. 363–69.

[7]   Kearney, J. 2010. "Food Consumption Trends and Drivers." *Philosophical Transactions of the Royal Society of London B: Biological Sciences* 365, no. 1554, pp. 2793–807.

[8]   Alexandratos, N., and J. Bruinsma. 2012. *World Agriculture Towards 2030/2050: The 2012 Revision*, 3, 12 vols. FAO, Rome: ESA Working paper.

[9]   Hoffman, D.J. 2001. "Obesity in Developing Countries: Causes and Implications." *Food Nutrition and Agriculture* 28, pp. 35–44.

[10] Pingali, P. 2007. "Westernization of Asian Diets and the Transformation of Food Systems: Implications for Research and Policy." *Food Policy* 32, no. 3, pp. 281–98.

[11] Regmi, A., and J. Dyck. 2001. "Effects of Urbanization on Global Food Demand." *Changing the Structure of Global Food Consumption and Trade*, pp. 23–30.

[12] Popkin, B. 2000. "Urbanization and the Nutrition Transition. Policy Brief 7 of 10." *Focus* 3. Achieving Urban Food and Nutrition Security in the Developing World.

[13] Knudsen, M.T., N. Halberg, J.E. Olesen, J. Byrne, V. Iyer, and N. Toly. 2006. "Global Trends in Agriculture and Food Systems." *In Global Development of Organic Agriculture-Challenges and Prospects*, 1–48. CABI Publishing.

[14] Vasileska, A., and G. Rechkoska. 2012. "Global and Regional Food Consumption Patterns and Trends." *Procedia-Social and Behavioral Sciences* 44, pp. 363–69.

[15] FAO, R. 2006. "Prospects for Food, Nutrition, Agriculture, and Major Commodity Groups." *World Agriculture: Towards*, 2030, 2050.

[16] Nishida, C., R. Uauy, S. Kumanyika, and P. Shetty. 2004. "The Joint WHO/FAO Expert Consultation on Diet, Nutrition and the Prevention of Chronic Diseases: Process, Product and Policy Implications." *Public Health Nutrition* 7, no. 1a, pp. 245–50.

[17] Food Scarcity-Trends, Challenges, Solutions. http://saiplatform.org/uploads/Modules/Library/Dexia%20AM%20Research%20Food%20Scarcity.pdf

[18] Boutayeb, A., and S. Boutayeb. 2005. "The Burden of Noncommunicable Diseases in Developing Countries." *International Journal for Equity in Health* 4, no. 1, p. 2.

[19] https://ers.usda.gov/data-products/ag-and-food-statistics-charting-the-essentials/ag-and-food-sectors-and-the-economy/

[20] Prentice, A.M. 2005. "The Emerging Epidemic of Obesity in Developing Countries." *International Journal of Epidemiology* 35, no. 1, pp. 93–99.

[21] Doak, C.M., L.S. Adair, C. Monteiro, and B.M. Popkin. 2000. "Overweight and Underweight Coexist within Households in Brazil, China, and Russia." *The Journal of Nutrition* 130, no. 12, pp. 2965–71.

[22] Pretty, J. 2002. "People, Livelihoods and Collective Action in Biodiversity Management." *Biodiversity, Sustainability, and Human com.*

[23] Knudsen, M.T., N. Halberg, J.E. Olesen, J. Byrne, V. Iyer, and N. Toly. 2006. "Global Trends in Agriculture and Food Systems." *In Global Development of Organic Agriculture-Challenges and Prospects*, 1–48. CABI Publishing.

[24] The Future Trends of Food and Challenges. 2017. *Food and Agriculture Organization of the United Nations Rome.*

[25] VAN ES, H. A. R. O. L. D., and J. WOODARD. *Innovation in Agriculture and Food Systems in the Digital Age.*

[26] Kendall, H.W., and D. Pimentel. 1994. "Constraints on the Expansion of the Global Food Supply." *Ambio*, pp. 198–205.

[27] Breman, H., J.R. Groot, and H. van Keulen. 2001. "Resource Limitations in Sahelian Agriculture." *Global Environmental Change* 11, no. 1, pp. 59–68.

[28] Wolfe, A. H., and J.A. Patz. 2002. "Reactive Nitrogen and Human Health: Acute and Long-Term Implications." *Ambio: A Journal of the Human Environment* 31, no. 2, pp. 120–25.

[29] Environmental Indicators for Agriculture. 2001. "Methods and Results." *Agriculture and Food*, 400, 3 vols. France: OECD Publications Service.

[30] Global Panel on Agriculture and Food Systems for Nutrition. 2016.

[31] Desa, U. 2015. "World Population Prospects: The 2015 Revision, Key Findings, and Advance Tables." Working Paper No.

CHAPTER 3

Healthcare and the Life Sciences

1. The Rapidly Growing Burden of Healthcare
2. Toward the Globalization of the Healthcare Industry
3. The Digitization of Healthcare
4. Toward a Personalized, Precise, and Robotic Medicine
5. The Potential of Nano-Medicine
6. Continued Upsurge in the Medication Expenditure
7. The Rise of Chronic and Non-Communicable Diseases

The Rapidly Growing Burden of Healthcare

Over the course of the past 50 years, life expectancy at birth has been growing progressively across the world, from an average of 46.5 years in 1955 to 65.2 years in 2002 [1]. While there are significant disparities between developed and developing economies, the risk of death between ages 15 years and 60 years has dropped from 35.4 percent in 1955 to 20.7 percent in 2002 across the world [1]. In the next four decades, developed economies will have the oldest population structures, but the fastest aging populations and massive majority of older people will reside in less developed economies. The aging population trend has existed in developed economies for many decades, but is growing fast in developing economies. The increasing levels of life expectancy combined with the swelling aging populations involve significant implications for health, including increased rates of non-communicable diseases, shortages of healthcare workers or resources, and growing numbers of people needing long-term care. As a direct consequence of aging populations, the incidence of chronic or non-communicable diseases is on the constant rise. In 2010, chronic diseases accounted for 86 percent of all U.S. health expenditure. Other parts of the world and even developing economies are on the same path and will be affected by the financial burden of chronic or non-communicable diseases [2]. In addition to aging populations, unhealthy diets and sedentary lifestyles have become pervasive in recent years and are causing non-communicable diseases or disorders such as diabetes, atherosclerosis, and obesity. For example, across the world, 382 million people are categorized as diabetic and 600 million as obese [3].

The impacts of aging populations, rising levels of life expectancy, and higher incidence of non-communicable diseases on healthcare systems, workforce, and public budgets will be enormous. Concerns about the sustainability of healthcare systems are growing, as costs seem to be running out of control in many Western countries. In the United States, the Medicare Trust Fund is projected to have difficulty in the coming years. In France, the healthcare system, ranked as the best in the world by the World Health Organization in 2000, is on the verge of ruin [4]. In England, the healthcare system is suffering from huge deficits. By 2020, healthcare expenditure is expected to account for 21 percent of the gross domestic product (GDP) in the United States and a median of 16 percent of GDP in other OECD countries [5]. Spending on healthcare regularly grows faster than GDP does; therefore, the share of healthcare expenditure in the GDP is set to grow over time in most Western countries. According to the World Health Organization (WHO), global health expenditure has been growing by an average of 6 percent per year since 1995, which is 2 percent above the growth of global GDP for the past four decades [6]. The global healthcare expenditure may reach a colossal amount of 9.3 trillion U.S. dollars in coming years [7]. The U.S. health spending increased from 13.1 percent of GDP in 2000 to 17.1 percent in 2010, and the number may reach 20 percent of the GDP by 2020 and 28 percent by 2050. All these indicators point to the conclusion that healthcare costs are rising too fast across the globe. Along with aging populations, there are serious concerns about the decreasing proportions of populations who will be paying into publicly funded healthcare systems. The increasing incidence of chronic diseases is directly correlated with age levels; therefore, a large number of healthcare services are dedicated to elderly people. For example, in the United States, only 5 percent of the patients account for almost half of the healthcare expenses. The financial burden of healthcare services is aggravated by a global shortage of clinicians [8]. The number of medical professionals, including medical doctors and nurses, is falling in real terms in many countries, despite the rising demand. In order to remedy the shortages of healthcare professionals, some countries seek to fill the gap by recruiting doctors and nurses from other countries, thus depriving the home countries of their healthcare professionals [8].

The socioeconomic development, particularly in emerging countries, has led to global improved health, but at higher costs for both citizens and governments. In the last three decades, the global health expenditure has been growing faster than the global GDP, and this trend is expected to exacerbate in the near future [9]. In the past few years, the expenditure and quality of healthcare have risen together, but there is no guarantee that this correlation will continue in the future [9]. Healthcare is perhaps the only industry that has not seen a significant improvement in labor productivity from technology yet. In contrast to other industries, healthcare is characterized by an emphasis on expert labor without any technology automation. Due to the rising costs of healthcare, many countries are taking measures to reform their public healthcare programs, including access to healthcare services, use of electronic medical records, and payments. The advances in information technology and rising costs have contributed to the increasing empowerment of healthcare consumers over time. The consumers are more informed about the quality of healthcare services and are raising their expectations accordingly. The more educated and affluent consumers expect a high-quality service, a personalized care, and a coordinated and efficient treatment form their care providers [9].

Toward the Globalization of the Healthcare Industry

While manufacturing and many service sectors, including insurance, banking, investment, and software, have been globalized, the healthcare industry has remained largely local. There are indications that this is going to change. The increasing expenditure of the healthcare sector is pushing businesses, consumers, and policymakers to take advantage of globalization efficiencies, as no country has all the healthcare endowments.

In the past two decades between 1990 and 2010, national health systems considered a variety of global solutions to their local problems, including the exchange of skilled workers, nurses, and physicians. For instance, the United States and the United Kingdom recruited a large number of Filipino, Caribbean, and South African nurses [10]. These exchanges were beneficial to both home and host countries, as the migrant nurses from the Philippines could earn up to nine times in the United Kingdom what they would earn at home [11]. Similarly, a large number of medical professionals and graduates in the United States were employed from low-cost countries such as India, Pakistan, the Philippines, and other English-speaking countries. By some estimates, about 25 percent of the American physicians have received their training in foreign medical schools [36]. The globalization of healthcare is not limited to the United States and the United Kingdom. The healthcare systems in more than 50 countries, including Australia, Brazil, Sweden, Malaysia, and the UAE, are relying more and more on foreign professionals [12]. Consistent with this trend, the global pharmaceutical companies are going global and continue to develop new drugs in multiple countries. As they are dispersing their research and development operations across the globe, more clinical trials are done in low-cost countries such as India. In the quest for more efficiency and lower cost, some American hospitals have turned to companies in Australia, Israel, India, Switzerland, and Lebanon to decode their CT scans overnight. Another aspect of global convergence in healthcare is related to the communication and implementation of best practices as the barriers among pharmaceuticals, providers, clinicians, biotech, and payers are lowered.

As more advanced technologies are allowing a more efficient exchange of information across the globe, both healthcare providers and receivers are being affected. The global expansion of pharmaceutical companies necessitates some globally harmonized regulations and standards. Furthermore, health executives need information, metrics, and transparency to streamline decision-making. This issue is of prime importance in countries with higher tax rates that benefit from a universal healthcare because citizens demand more transparency about public finances and how their taxes are spent. The globalization of healthcare is in its early stages, but it is expected to significantly grow in the near future. The globalization of the healthcare industry creates huge opportunities for large corporations, but at the same time, may involve major threats to consumers and national healthcare systems. Swollen costs, uneven or low-quality service, and unfair access are among some of these threats.

The Digitization of Healthcare

Despite some remarkable scientific breakthroughs, healthcare services are lagging behind in digitization in comparison with other industries. The introduction of digital technologies is expected to substantially transform the healthcare industry in the next two decades. However, the digitization of the healthcare industry may face major regulatory and economic barriers. Consumers' desire to use digital healthcare services is not always well responded by the industry, as two-thirds of the U.S. physicians are still unwilling to allow patients to access their own health records [13]. Nevertheless, the push for digitization is coming mainly from the rising cost of health services due to global aging populations and new treatment procedures. Even maintaining the existing level of service necessitates more efficiencies that are feasible only via digitization.

Two major trends in the industry will be a disruption to the location of care and disruption to the type of care [14]. The disruption to the location of healthcare involves moving care out of the hospital and put it closer to home. On another hand, the disruption to the type of care involves more prevention and management of diseases than their diagnostic and treatment. A digital healthcare will focus rather on the prevention and management of diseases. As a result, consumers will be responsible for handling their own health at home. These changes involve fewer visits of physicians at hospitals. Digital technologies will enable patients to monitor and track their vital signs and receive a virtual care consultation and medical advice without leaving their homes. This degree of autonomy and self-sufficiency will tremendously reduce the cost of healthcare services. At the same time, digital health-related services are marked by higher accuracy, as they are data-driven and are likely to be more successful [15].

Virtual care will extend access to healthcare in remote areas and will create a new structure for the healthcare system. As a result, there will be less focus on building new beds and more on developing digital services to provide improved access at lower cost. The digitization will lead to an emphasis on consumer-centric healthcare, thus enabling citizens to assume more responsibility for managing their healthcare. In this new model, the consumers will play an important role in using digital tools to improve productivity by reducing the need for professionals. Moreover, the use of precision medicine, robotics, and medical printing will improve patients' healthcare services at a lower cost. Digitization will move healthcare closer to the home, through advances in the connected home and virtual care, and will empower consumers to assume more responsibility in managing their healthcare. In addition, digitization will lead the healthcare enterprises to provide data-driven solutions and make decisions more effectively. Therefore, digitization is expected to create a major shift toward a value-based healthcare where the gap between the digital and physical worlds is bridged [15].

Data captured by wearable devices, mobile health apps (mHealth), and social media can be used to transform healthcare. The global digital health market, including wireless health, electronic medical records, and telehealth, was estimated at 60.8 billion U.S. dollars in 2013 and is expected to increase to 233.3 billion U.S. dollars by 2020. Five fastest growing segments of the digital health market include telemedicine, mobile health, electronic patient records, wearables, and social media. Among all sectors, telemedicine is the fastest-growing segment with 315 percent year-over-year growth from 2013 to 2014. Digitization is marked by revolutionizing companies offering health kiosks and mobile applications where patients can video conference with physicians, who can also access their personal medical records. For example, HealthTap, an interactive health company, aims at reinventing the healthcare services by incorporating both patients and doctors over the Internet via applications for iPhone, iPad, and Android. It has built a large network of more than 100,000 physicians and 10 million active users [16]. HealthTap offers professional services to subscribers who can consult with a physician 24 hours a day seven days a week. Similarly, Teladoc uses the telephone and videoconferencing to offer on-demand remote medical care via mobile devices, the Internet, video, and phone [17]. More than half of the U.S. states recognize virtual healthcare, as they require health insurers to treat virtual care services as equivalent to face-to-face consultations when reimbursing their customers [15].

Toward a Personalized, Precise, and Robotic Medicine

Traditionally, medical treatments have been developed to work on average persons; however, the outcomes of a treatment can substantially vary from one individual to another. A treatment that is beneficial to one patient could be ineffective or even dangerous for other patients. Approximately 30 to 40 percent of the patients take medications for which the negative effects outweigh the benefits. Along with digitization, advances in genomics sequencing, cloud computing, and analytics are leading to the rise of precision medicine, which aims at adapting medical treatments to an individual's genetic profile and lifestyle. In other words, personalized or precision medicine takes into consideration a patient's lifestyle, genes, and environment to improve disease prevention, diagnosis, and management altogether. Currently, we are at the threshold of a new phase of medical transformation where the new technological advances are allowing the development of targeted treatments. Precision medicine may offer digital diagnostic tools or companion devices. Consistent with this trend, the revenues of businesses focusing on genomics sequencing and data analytics such as Illumina have been soaring [15]. The concept of precision medicine is widely employed to fight cancer by genomic-profiling tests [18]. It is estimated that 60 percent of the patients could benefit from genomics sequencing and data analytics in the next decade [19]. More recently, the new advances in robotics have created multiple applications for medical purposes, allowing complex procedures in surgery. Such procedures not only will improve treatment outcomes, but also will substantially lower the cost of healthcare.

Robot-assisted surgery dates back to 30 years ago, but it is increasingly gaining popularity in the past decade. Robots enable minimally invasive procedures, and thus reduce the chance of infection, pain, and blood loss. Often, robot-assisted surgeries benefit from faster recovery and fewer complications. Robot-assisted surgeries combined with virtual devices may allow surgeons to connect with their patients remotely. Surgeons can control the robotic arms while sitting at a computer console near the operating table. Currently, the global medical robotics market is estimated to be worth approximately six billion U.S. dollars and is growing fast [20]. In 2014, Da Vinci robots were used in more than 500,000 surgical operations around the world [21]. In addition to surgical operations, the advanced robots may be used in a variety of healthcare services, including diagnostics and medication. For instance, the Chinese Internet giant Baidu.com is offering an application that uses voice recognition to make instant diagnostic suggestions based on a list of symptoms that users enter into their phones. The early diagnostic may guide the users or patients to the most appropriate healthcare professionals in their communities [22].

3D printing is another emerging technology that is becoming popular in personalized medicine. 3D printing is experiencing large growth and is expected to reach 12 billion U.S. dollars in 2018 [23]. The 3D technology has been applied in different areas of healthcare, including hearing aids, facial reconstruction, personal prosthetics, dental crowns, and surgical implants. The advances in 3D printing are leading to new applications in drug production and medical devices manufacturing. The 3D printing technology is often used to manufacture customized and smart medical implants [24]. The main advantage of 3D printing is that the implants, prostheses, pills, and biological structures are becoming more personalized, as they are tailored to individuals' differences. At the same time, the 3D technology enables manufacturing within hospitals or healthcare facilities, and thus reduces long waits or expensive costs.

The Potential of Nano-Medicine

Nanotechnology consists of the processing of, separation, consolidation, and deformation of materials by one atom or one molecule [25]. Due to their unique properties, nanomaterials are receiving a good deal of attention from health and life sciences. Many applications from cell imaging to therapeutics for cancer treatment and biomedical procedures can benefit from nanotechnology. Nanomaterials may gain functionalities by interfacing with biological molecules or structures and can be applied in vivo and in vitro biomedical research. Increasingly, nanomaterials are used in diagnostic devices, analytical tools, physical therapy applications, and drug-delivery vehicles [25]. All these features have led to a new perspective in medicine labeled as nano-medicine. Nanomaterials can provide medications into specific parts of the human body, thus making the medications more effective and less harmful to the other organs of the body.

Nanoparticles can be used to enhance MRI and ultrasound results in bio-medical applications of in vivo imaging, as they contain metals whose properties are dramatically altered. Nanoparticles are useful in diagnostics and treatment of soft-tissue tumors because they absorb the energy and heat up enough to kill the cancer cells. The specific targeting will enable medical professionals to selectively reduce the overall drug consumption and its side-effects. Furthermore, certain nanoparticles may prolong the life and effects of drugs inside the body.

In surgical operations, nanotechnology can be used to build tiny surgical instruments and robots in order to execute microsurgeries on any part of the body. In other words, nanotechnology can be applied to perform minuscule, targeted, and accurate surgical operations, without damaging a significant part of the body. Nano-robots or minuscule robots can be introduced into the patient's body to perform treatment on a cellular level. The visualization and control of such surgeries will be done via computers and nano-instruments, which are expected to reduce the chances of a mistake and human error significantly. Furthermore, nanotechnology may be used to produce artificially stimulated cells in order to repair damaged tissues and cells. The tissue engineering capacity can replace conventional treatments, transplantation of organs, and artificial implants [25]. Nanorobotic phagocytes or artificial white blood cells using nanotechnology can be injected into the bloodstream to create a synthetic immune system against pathogenic microbes, viruses, and fungi. Nanorobotic phagocytes can fight the deadliest infectious without negative effects on the patient. They are more effective and faster than antibiotic-aided natural phagocytes. Similar techniques can be used to selectively destroy cancerous cells, clear obstructions from the bloodstream, and prevent ischemic damage in the event of a stroke [25].

Continued Upsurge in the Medication Expenditure

The global spending on medicines is growing around 6 percent per year and is expected to reach nearly 1.5 trillion U.S. dollars by 2021. The United States is the largest pharmaceutical market, growing by 6 to 9 percent over the next five years. Currently, China is the second largest pharmaceutical market, but the shares of emerging countries are growing faster

[26]. As a general trend, developed economies are gradually descending, whereas developing and emerging countries are climbing the rankings of medicine spending. This trend has continued for the past decades and is likely to continue over the next two decades. The 10 largest developed markets for medication consist of the United States, Japan, Germany, the United Kingdom, Italy, France, Spain, Canada, South Korea, and Australia. Likewise, China, Brazil, Russia, India, Mexico, and Turkey are the largest developing pharmaceutical markets [26]. The global amount spent on medicines could double over the next 15 years. The drivers of such growth include oncology with 120 to 135 billion U.S. dollars and diabetes treatments with 95 to 110 billion U.S. dollars. Furthermore, biologic treatments for autoimmune diseases are expected to continue to see increasing usage across the globe and will reach 75 to 90 billion U.S. dollars in spending by 2021. The difference between developed and developing markets spending is that the formers spend on original brands, while the developing markets are attracted to non-original products [26].

Medications are already very expensive in the United States, but their prices are likely to surge even higher in the coming years. Based on a study conducted between January 2006 and December 2015, retail prices for 113 chronic-use brand-name drugs increased cumulatively over 10 years by an average of 188.7 percent [27]. The high cost of prescription drugs puts a heavy financial burden on healthcare systems, insurers, patients, employers, and providers. In 2015, the average senior American taking 4.5 prescription drugs per month had to pay more than 26,000 U.S. dollars per year for the cost of therapy [27]. Among the industrialized countries, the United States has the highest spending on prescription drugs [28]. The prescription drug expenditure constitutes nearly 20 percent of the healthcare costs, showing a growth of 13.1 percent in 2014 [29]. In recent years, specialty drugs are rapidly gaining acceptance and popularity in the United States. Specialty drugs are difficult to administer and often come in injectable formulations. Originally, specialty drugs were used exclusively to treat chronic diseases such as cancer, rheumatoid arthritis, and multiple sclerosis, but in the last few years, their application has expanded to touch additional diseases [31]. Specialty drugs are generally expensive and accounted for 36 percent of the total drug spending in the United States in 2015, or approximately 155 billion U.S. dollars of the 428 billion U.S. dollars spent annually on medicines. Spending for specialty drugs has grown by 23 percent between 2014 and 2015, compared to growth of 7.8 percent for traditional medicines. Along with this trend, specialty pharmacies are expanding rapidly. Specialty pharmacies are intended to manage the necessary handling, storage, and distribution of complex therapy drugs [30].

Some drug makers have seen their reputation tarnished by scandals and reports on predatory pricing and unethical practices. For example, Pfizer Inc. has raised prices on 133 of its drugs in the United States in 2016 by 10 percent or more. Sovaldi, a drug to treat Hepatitis C virus, costs 1,000 U.S. dollars per day for the 12-week course of treatment. Orkambi, a drug therapy intended to treat cystic fibrosis, costs 259,000 U.S. dollars per year [32]. Due to these hefty prices, many countries are introducing price controls by putting pressure on pharmaceutical companies. In the United States, health plans control medication pricing, while in the United Kingdom and Germany, more regulations have been adopted to control drugs prices [33]. In tandem with tighter controls on prices, the effectiveness of drugs is evaluated in many countries like the United Kingdom and China. In China, the government is bringing the medications under a central supervision. In developing economies such as India, pricing authorities are controlling medication prices for a wide range of drugs, including painkillers and antibiotics, and drugs for cancer and skin disease treatments. Due to an increasing demand and rising prices, generic drugs will continue to gain market share as consumers seek to reduce costs. While in the United States, generic medications account for 70 percent of the prescription drugs by volume, in China, they account for two-thirds of prescriptions.

The Rise of Chronic and Non-Communicable Diseases

Aging populations coupled with the improving hygiene and healthcare levels are causing the phenomenal rise of non-communicable or chronic diseases across the globe. Other factors such as unhealthy diets, tobacco and alcohol addiction, environmental degradation, genetically modified organisms, dependence on smartphones, and sedentary lifestyles contribute to the upsurge of non-communicable diseases. The main types of non-communicable diseases are associated with older age and include cardiovascular diseases, cancers, chronic respiratory diseases and asthma, diabetes, and mental disorders. Obesity is an important risk factor for many non-communicable diseases and conditions, including stroke, heart disease, cancer, and arthritis. The total number of people with diabetes is 387 million and is expected to increase to 592 million by 2035, according to the International Diabetes Federation. China and India have the largest number of diabetes sufferers in the world, at more than 96 million and 66 million, respectively.

In the next decade, people in every world region will suffer more death and disability from such non-communicable diseases than from infectious and parasitic diseases. In 2008, non-communicable diseases accounted for 86 percent of the diseases in high-income countries, 65 percent in middle-income countries, and 37 percent in low-income countries. By 2030, the shares of non-communicable diseases in middle- and low-income countries will increase, respectively, to 75 and 50 percent. According to the WHO, non-communicable diseases are responsible for the death of 40 million people each year, representing 70 percent of all deaths. Cardiovascular diseases with 17.7 million deaths per year account for most deaths followed by cancers (8.8 million), respiratory diseases (3.9 million), and diabetes (1.6 million).

Non-communicable diseases imply some serious social and economic consequences. At the individual level, non-communicable diseases lead the patients and their families to poverty, pain, and bankruptcy. It is estimated that about 100 million patients in the world fall into poverty every year due to the costs associated with their treatment [6]. Many organizations are affected adversely, as their workforce lose productivity or are eliminated. The World Economic Forum studies (2008) estimated that the emerging economies such as Brazil, China, India, South Africa, and Russia might have lost more than 20 million productive life-years due to cardiovascular diseases in 2000. Obviously, the impact of all types of non-communicable diseases in the future will be much more significant, as the number of patients continues to grow drastically. The economic losses of non-communicable diseases could reach 47 trillion U.S. dollars in the next two decades, hindering the economic growth and prosperity across the world.

Mental disorders such as dementia and Alzheimer's are other prevalent non-communicable diseases that are affecting the lives of a large number of people and are often associated with old age. Dementia could have various causes and symptoms, but this disease is often associated with a loss of memory, reasoning, and other cognitive capacities [34]. Dementia, especially in its early stages, is difficult to diagnose, and very frequently, it remains undiagnosed and under-reported even in developed economies. For that reason, the data about the prevalence of dementia across the world are not standard and reliable. Based on the Organization for Economic Cooperation and Development (OECD) reports in 2000, dementia affected about 10 million people in OECD member countries, representing 7 percent of the people aged 65 years or older. Alzheimer's disease is the most common form of dementia and accounted for between two-fifths and four-fifths of all dementia cases. Currently, the number of people affected by dementia is estimated between 27 and 36 million across the world [34]. The prevalence of dementia is very low at a younger age, but increases sharply after age 65 years. Based on the OECD studies, only 3 percent of the people between ages 65 and 69 years were affected by dementia, while the proportion for those between 85 and 89 years reached 30 percent. Similar studies in France and Germany showed that more than half of women aged 90 years or older had some forms of dementia [34]. The studies by the Alzheimer's Disease International suggest that, by 2050, there will be around 115 million people worldwide living with Alzheimer's or dementia [34]. As the world's population is getting older, the number of affected people is expected to put mounting pressure on healthcare providers, families, and governments across the world. According to the World Alzheimer Report, the total worldwide cost of dementia was estimated at more than 600 billion U.S. dollars in 2010 [34]. The cost associated with dementia is expected to rise exponentially, especially in low- and middle-income countries that have insufficient resources for mental health allocating less than 2 percent of their health budget to the treatment and prevention of this disease [35]. Most of the people affected by dementia eventually lose their independence and need constant help with their daily activities causing a heavy economic and social burden on their families and communities [35]. As families become smaller and people have fewer children, there will be fewer family members to look after elderly people affected by mental disorders.

References

[1]   World Health Organization. 2003. "Global Health: Today's Challenges." *The World Health Report.*

[2]   http://nature.com/articles/nm1212-1719?WT.ec_id=NM-201212

[3]   Garrett, L. 2013. *Existential Challenges to Global Health.* Center on International Cooperation.

[4]   Campos, L. 2009. "That was the Synthetic Biology that was." In *Synthetic Biology*, 5–21. Springer, Dordrecht.

[5]   PricewaterhouseCoopers, L.L.P. 2005. *HealthCast 2020: Creating a Sustainable Future.* New York, NY: PricewaterhouseCoopers.

[6]   https://aicpa.org/research/cpahorizons2025/globalforces/downloadabledocuments/

[7]   http://trust.org/alertnet/news/funding-cuts-imperil-european-fight-against-tb-hiv/ And http://ghd-net.org/sites/default/files/Health percent20 Diplomacy percent20Monitorpercent20Volume percent203 percent20Issue percent204.pdf

[8]   Healthcare Challenges and Trends: The Patient at the Heart of Care, https://cgi.com/sites/default/files/white-papers/cgi-health-challenges-white-paper.pdf

[9]   Garrett, L. 2013. *Existential Challenges to Global Health.* Center on International Cooperation.

[10] "Getting Creative: Nursing Recruiters Leave No Stone Unturned." by Jose Latour, U.S. Visa News. June 28, 2001. "Foreign Nurses Arrive to Help Baby Boomers." by Ahmar Mustikhan, Shreveport Times, July 10, 2005; "U.S. Ready to Absorb 3,500 New Pinoy Nurses." *Manila Standard*, July 23, 2005.

[11] Sison, M. 2003. *Philippines: Health System Suffers a Brain Drain.* Migration Stories.

[12] IFC Global Conference, 2005. *Investing in Private Healthcare in Emerging Markets Conference: International Finance Corporation (IFC).* February 16–18, 2005. Washington, DC.

[13] Munro, D. 2015. "New Poll Shows Two-Thirds of Doctors Reluctant to Share Health Data With Patients." *Forbes*, June 8, 2015. http://forbes.com/sites/danmunro/2015/06/08/two%E2%80%92thirds-of-doctors-are-reluctant-to-sharehealth-data-with-patients/

[14] Christensen, C. 2008. *The Innovator's Prescription: A Disruptive Solution for Health Care.* McGraw-Hill.

[15] World Economic Forum White Paper Digital Transformation of Industries: In Collaboration with Accenture, 2016. http://reports.weforum.org/digital-transformation/wp-content/blogs.dir/94/mp/files/pages/files/digital-enterprise-narrative-final-january-2016.pdf

[16] Lapowsky, I. 2014. "HealthTap's Video Chatting Doctors Want to End Your WebMD Meltdowns." *Wired*, July 30, 2014. http://wired.com/2014/07/healthtap-prime/

[17] Wieczner, J. September 24, 2014. "Thanks to Obamacare, Virtual-Reality Doctors are Booming." *Fortune*, Retrieved June 28, 2015.

[18] Foundation Medicine. 2015. "Our Vision." http://foundationmedicine.com/

[19] UnitedHealth Center for Health Reform & Modernization. March 2012. "Personalized Medicine: Trends and Prospects for the New Science of Genetic Testing and Molecular Diagnostics." Working Paper 7, http://unitedhealthgroup.com/~/media/UHG/PDF/2012/UNH-Working-Paper-7.ashx

[20] "Global Medical Robotics Market Outlook 2018." *PRNewswire*, May 4, 2015. http://prnewswire.com/newsreleases/global-medical-robotics-market-outlook-2018-300077013.html

[21] Personalized Medicine: Trends and prospects for the new science of genetic testing and molecular diagnostics", UnitedHealth Center for Health Reform & Modernization, Working Paper 7, March 2012, http://www.unitedhealthgroup.com/~/media/UHG/PDF/2012/UNH-Working-Paper-7.ashx.

[22] Bergen, M. 2015. "Baidu's 'Medical Robot': Chinese Search Engine Reveals Its AI for Health." *Re/code*, August 9, 2015. http://recode.net/2015/08/09/baidus-medical-robot-chinese-voice-diagnostic-app/

[23] Columbus, L. 2015. "2015 Roundup of 3D Printing Market Forecasts and Estimates." *Forbes*, March 31, 2015. http://forbes.com/sites/louiscolumbus/2015/03/31/2015-roundup-of-3d-printing-market-forecasts-and-estimates/

[24] Krauskopf, L. 2015. "Cheaper Robots Could Replace More Factory Workers: Study." *Reuters*, February 9, 2015. http://reuters.com/article/2015/02/10/us-manufacturers-robots-idUSKBN0LE00720150210

[25] Abeer, S. 2012. "Future Medicine: Nanomedicine." *JIMSA*, 25, pp. 187–92.

[26] "Outlook for Global Medicines through 2021." *Balancing Cost and Value*, http://static.correofarmaceutico.com/docs/2016/12/12/qiihi_outlook_for_global_medicines_through_2021.pdf

[27] Schondelmeyer, S.W., and L. Purvis. 2016. *Trends in Retail Prices of Brand Name Prescription Drugs Widely Used by Older Americans, 2006 to 2015.*

[28] Quon, B.S., R. Firszt, and M.J. Eisenberg. 2005. "A Comparison of Brand-Name Drug Prices Between Canadian-Based Internet Pharmacies and Major US Drug Chain Pharmacies." *Ann Intern Med* 143, no. 6, pp. 397–403.

[29] Safran, D.G., P. Neuman, C. Schoen, M.S. Kitchman, I.B. Wilson, B. Cooper, and W.H. Rogers. 2005. "Prescription Drug Coverage and

Seniors: Findings from a 2003 National Survey: Where Do Things Stand on the Eve of Implementing the New Medicare Part D Benefit?" *Health Affairs* 24, no. Suppl1, pp. W5–152.

[30] "Emerging Trends in the Specialty Drug Industry." 2016. https://elsevier.com/clinical-solutions/insights/resources/insights-articles/drug-information/emerging-trends-in-the-specialty-drug-industry

[31] Koons, C. October, 2015. *Pfizer Raised Prices on 133 Drugs This Year, And It's Not Alone.* Bloomberg.

[32] Appleby, J. May 2014. *Who Should Get Pricey Hepatitis C Drugs?* Kaiser Health News.

[33] Task Force on Community Prevention Services. 2015. "Preventing Excessive Alcohol Consumption." *The Guide to Community Preventive Services Website.* http://thecommunityguide.org/alcohol/index.html

[34] World Health Organization. 2011. *Global Health and Aging.* Geneva: World Health Organization.

[35] Jonas, O.B. 2014. "Global Health Threats of the 21st Century." *Finance & Development* 51, no. 4.

[36] http://time.com/4658651/medical-school-foreign-doctors-study

PART II
Business Transformations

CHAPTER 4

The Sharing Economy

Rise of Sharing Economy

Sharing economy or the collaborative economy is an important global trend that is leading us beyond what we have experienced as consumers, workers, owners, and communities. It is based on our ability to share our possessions, services, and needs. It affects many industries, including hospitality, tourism, transport, and lending. More importantly, sharing economy is driven by multiple technological, social, cultural, and economic forces. As Amazon.com and eBay capitalized on the connectivity of the Internet to create e-commerce business models in the 1990s, some companies such as Uber and Airbnb are currently harnessing the convenience of mobile technologies and wireless connectivity to construct new business patterns. By analogy, we may suggest that, as Amazon.com and eBay revolutionized the meaning of retail, logistics, reading, and shopping, the sharing economy businesses are poised to change the meaning of possession, consumption, work, and enterprise. Sharing economy businesses have witnessed a spectacular rise in recent years and are expected to continue their phenomenal growth in the next decade. The sharing economy is growing steadily by incorporating more sectors and its size could grow from roughly 15 billion U.S. dollars in 2017 to around 335 billion U.S. dollars by 2025 [1]. According to the Pew Research Center survey of 4,787 American adults in 2016, 72 percent have used some kind of shared or on-demand service. Likewise, Owyang et al. [2] reported that 29 percent of the British population had engaged at least once in a sharing transaction, and 23 percent had used one or more platforms such as Airbnb, Uber, TaskRabbit, Etsy, and Kickstarter. Based on other estimates, in 2014, 25 percent of the United Kingdom population shared online services [3]. According to Goudin [4], the potential economic gain due to the sharing economy is estimated at around 572 billion euros in annual consumption across the European Union. Uber and Airbnb are innovative companies that were founded less than 10 years ago, but currently have operations in a large number of countries across the world. As the most valuable startup, Uber operates in 600 cities across 78 countries, has 75 million monthly active riders and three million active drivers, and offers an astonishing 15 million rides a day [24]. Uber provided four billion rides in 2017, and this number is expected to grow fast in the coming months. Airbnb is another pioneer of the sharing economy, with an online platform that matches room seekers to homeowners. Founded in 2008, Airbnb currently operates in more than 65,000 cities and 191 countries [25]. With less than 600 employees, Airbnb has a million properties listed for rent, making it larger than the world's biggest hotel chains. Airbnb was valued at 31 billion U.S. dollars in May 2017. Uber and Airbnb are indicators of a burgeoning trend toward what is termed as sharing or collaborative economy. The business model of Uber and Airbnb can be applied to any other unutilized or under-utilized asset or service, including bicycles, apartments, vacation homes, tools, designer clothes, accessories, objects of art, and yachts. With each month that passes, the impacts of sharing economy companies, including Uber and Airbnb, become more prevalent. The sharing economy business models can be applied to share goods, services, ideas, information, and skills through a network of individuals, and communities via computers and mobile apps. Despite their apparent differences, all these platforms match the supply and demand in a very accessible and low-cost way. In addition, these platforms create opportunities for buyers and sellers to interact, share feedback, and build mutual trust. Sharing economy releases the potential for peer-to-peer commerce across the globe by relying on the blockchain technology. Perhaps, the most important characteristic of sharing economy enterprises is that they create conditions to reduce the cost of producing each additional unit of good or service until the marginal cost tends toward zero. Interestingly, sharing activities can be for monetary or non-monetary benefits. As more businesses and consumers join the sharing economy, our societies and markets are undergoing drastic changes and disruptions. According to Time magazine, sharing economy is recognized as one of the top 10 trends that are expected to change the world. Some have compared the social and economic implications of sharing economy to those of the industrial revolution [5].

The Essence of Sharing Economy

The concept of sharing economy refers to different terms, including collaborative consumption, collaborative economy, on-demand economy, peer-to-peer economy, zero-marginal-cost economy, and crowd-based capitalism [6]. Sharing economy is based on collaboration and on-demand production or consumption. The sharing economy platforms offer opportunities, so people can share property, resources, time, and skills across online platforms. We may define sharing economy as an economic system built on sharing, swapping, trading, or renting products and services in a way that enables access over ownership, including business-to-consumer, business-to-business, and peer-to-peer transactions [7]. In other words, sharing and exchange of resources take place via information technology without any permanent transfer of ownership [8, 9]. According to Botsman [18], sharing economy is defined as "an economic system of decentralized networks and marketplaces that unlocks the value of underused assets by matching needs and haves, in ways that bypass traditional middlemen." Sharing economy businesses facilitate business-to-consumer or peer-to-peer transactions, can be for-profit or non-profit organizations, and range from small businesses to multi-billion giants such as Uber and Airbnb [1, 5]. The pivotal appeal of the sharing economy is a platform matching buyers and sellers and reducing transactions costs. The platform is generally operated separately from the services exchanged. The whole concept of sharing economy remains fuzzy and ambiguous, as it represents multiple business models that are undergoing constant transformation and innovation. In addition to the large for-profit businesses, there are a large number of small non-profit entities such as time banks, food swaps, repair collectives, makerspaces, and other grassroots organization [38, 10]. While the term *sharing* may imply altruistic or positive non-reciprocal social behavior, the services or goods exchanged in a sharing business model are often fee-paying in nature and involve economic benefits [11].

A New Economic Logic

According to Jeremy Rifkin, the sharing economy represents a paradigm shift that he labels the "third industrial revolution." [13]. The sharing economy represents a new economic paradigm because, by reducing and eliminating barriers such as ownership costs and inflexible distribution networks, it could allow greater access to crucial goods and services for people and communities [7]. The sharing economy seems particularly attractive when a large number of workers and consumers are under mounting pressure and are disappointed with the conventional economic model [7]. Under the current socioeconomic circumstances marked by the astonishing levels of inequality, sharing economy is beneficial for both workers and consumers, as they are enabled to act more independently, run their businesses, distribute their products and services, and democratize expensive assets. In this regard, the sharing economy could be viewed as a more humane model than the conventional economy with large-scale corporations and customers [7]. While the conventional economy is dominated by rivalry and opposition, the sharing economy is marked by common development and coordination. The platforms of the sharing economy do not exclude competition, but create economic value by increasing the number of participants on both sides of supply and demand [12]. The sharing economy is gradually transforming some fundamental concepts such as exchange, supply, demand, production, consumption, ownership, and transaction. The new logic of the sharing economy is different, as it is revolutionizing the very concept of production and economic value. It is suggested that the sharing economy hinges primarily on collaboration and altruism, and thus is a game-changing revolution to Western economics [1]. In other words, in the sharing economy, the participants do not pursue the goal of profit maximization; by contrast, self-interest is fulfilled through collaboration. The sharing economy represents a new mode of a market economy where Adam Smith's Economics of egoism is mitigated by altruism. What we have serves others and vice versa. As the number of market participants in the sharing economy increases, more assets are shared and more economic value is added [12]. The most important remark is that the sharing economy is changing the conventional economic model from competition to symbiosis and collaboration. This represents a paradigmatic shift where everyone is involved in production, distribution, and consumption. Furthermore, while the conventional economy focuses on the relationship between the market and government, the sharing economy considers a synergetic relationship between these two entities.

One of the most important features of the sharing economy is its reliance on a combination of new technologies, including data analytics, mobile connectivity, and cloud computing. Because of the recent advancements in telecommunication technology, the sharing economy can create a different type of economic value, which is different from the conventional economy. The created value in the sharing economy is more abstract, more complex, and more multidimensional than that of the conventional economy. Unlike the conventional economy, the sharing economy relies mainly on non-material factors to create value. This is a fundamental change because hard assets such as labor and land and even technology are not the only factors that determine economic growth. In other words, the growth of the sharing economy is derived from the intelligent combination of factors.

In the sharing economy, the creation of wealth depends on all parties who are participating in the supply, distribution, and consumption processes. The sharing economy covers a global marketplace where all producers and consumers across the world are in constant relationships. The created wealth in the sharing economy is social capital illustrated by trust, collaboration, and participation. Furthermore, in the sharing economy, rights and ownerships are separated, and as a result, exclusive products become sharable. In contrast to large and multi-level and large-scale organizations, the sharing economy creates a large number of micro-entrepreneurs who can directly run and manage their own businesses on a daily basis.

The sharing economy is distinguished from the normal economy by offering new modes of consumption, information, wealth, and humanization. The new mode of consumption means that, in the sharing economy, utilization is more important than ownership. The new mode of information implies that, in the sharing economy, resources across sectors are reallocated with high efficiency and low costs. The new mode of wealth means that, in the sharing economy, idle things, spiritual resources, cultural resources, and natural resources are shared. The new mode of humanization implies that, in the sharing economy, self-interest is achieved through altruism [12]. Based on these features, it is possible to claim that the sharing economy is a major economic and social force that could eventually revolutionize how we consume, how we work, how we do business, and how we interact with each other.

In conventional economies, the price is the result of a market competition where capital, land and other physical assets are accumulated to create and accumulate wealth. As a result, a minority of people take control of rare assets and exert their power over the rest of society. The race toward capital accumulation strains human relations, and people exclude each other. By contrast, the sharing economy breaks the structure of conventional economies by attaching value to utilization, rather than possession of assets and by generating wealth from increasing human relations. Trust acts as the building block of sharing economy and brings people together to create economic value. Therefore, the sharing economy makes us aware that we are all part of a social economic and ecological system with common interests and mutual relations, where we can benefit by being benefitted by others. In other words, the sharing economy can be seen as more humane and harmonious than the existing models of the conventional economy [14].

The sharing economy can be seen as an alternative to the dominant models of the 20th century such as the Keynesian and the neoliberal models, as it aims to embed economic dealings once again in social relations [15]. The notion of reciprocity originally is found in non-economic dealings of pre-modern societies and in groups such as families, clans, communities. The modern societies eliminated reciprocity by creating solid economic structures and monetary exchanges in commerce and labor. However, it seems that sharing economy again is reviving the notion of reciprocity in our post-modern societies by using advanced technologies to connect people [15].

The Drivers of Sharing Economy

Social Drivers

Currently, the world population is estimated at 7.7 billion and is expected to exceed eight billion in 2024, nine billion in 2038, and 10 billion in 2056. As the human population surges, the world resources become rarer. Therefore, a new economic paradigm such as sharing economy that relies on the utilization of assets, rather than their ownership can be considered as a sustainable and environment-friendly option. In addition to sustainability, the sharing economy creates opportunities for efficient utilization of assets and resources [16].

As the sharing economy promotes utilization, rather than ownership, it becomes very attractive to consumers [17]. As a result, both asset owners and consumers are able to reduce their costs and the number of resources needed. For instance, the average idle time of a car is 23 hours per day. When one car is put into sharing economy, it could reduce the sales of approximately eight cars. According to the former president of General Motors, every car joining the sharing economy may result in a reduction of production by 15 cars [12]. Unlike the conventional economy, in a sharing economy business, consumers have access to a large number of assets and services from a variety of brands, prices, and features. For example, the users of Airbnb have access to a wide range of accommodation options from a small room in a basement to luxurious mansions and middle-age castles.

The rise of the sharing economy is partly because of the transformation of social norms and cultural values. Across the world and particularly in the Western countries, people are getting more comfortable with strangers and trust them, so they can invite strangers into their home for dinner, share their home, vehicle, or vacation with them. Interestingly, as the trust in individuals is increased, the trust in government institutions and large corporations is diminished [18]. One may suggest that the trust that people put in government and large organizations is partially being replaced by the trust they put in their peers.

As the sharing economy creates business opportunities among strangers, it relies primarily on trust among market participants. The consumers must trust that the goods and services delivered via technological platforms will be as described. Indeed, sharing homes, cars, and lives requires a good degree of mutual trust between buyers and sellers. An important aspect of the sharing economy is that, instead of large corporations, governments, church, and other formal organizations, the consumers are putting their trust in strangers [19]. Consumers are free to choose among numerous brands of varying quality, regardless of advertisement, expert recommendations, and celebrity endorsements [17]. A peer evaluation and review system is designed, allowing the consumers to make informed decisions [16].

The sharing economy is a new form of communitarianism as the businesses match different consumers with each other and create opportunities for communication, socialization, and cultural exchange. This sense of community is an important driving force behind the sharing economy models, as the new generations are increasingly living in isolation and seek opportunities for human contact and personal interaction. The sharing economy models can bring people together in ways that conventional businesses do not [14].

The Environmental Awareness

As environmental degradation is becoming a pressing issue, a majority of citizens, particularly the youth, are advocating business practices that are not pernicious to the environment. This new wave of environmental awareness has been a driving force behind the collaborative consumption that emphasizes utilization, rather than full ownership. For instance, the idea of owning a car might become unattractive in the future, as many consumers will focus on getting a ride or renting a car instead of buying it [12]. The sharing economy is a green economy par excellence because it can reduce the substantial amounts of waste created from unused or underused resources.

Sharing and Happiness

By linking happiness to material possession, the conventional economy creates a vicious circle that often leads to human isolation, alienation, and mental disorder. The post-industrial cultural values imply that there is no direct relation between material wealth and happiness. Rather, they claim that happiness should be sought in socialization and collaboration with others. Indeed, some evidence confirms that the growth of the gross domestic product (GDP) in many countries, including the United States, China, and South Korea, has led to increasing levels of unhappiness, mental disorders, and depression [12]. The sharing economy provides opportunities for a citizen to interact with each other and experience kindness, which is often absent from the conventional businesses. For instance, one may share their spare room for socializing with people from other cultures [12].

Economic Drivers

In the past three decades, many western economies have been under-performing, and the inequality has been growing. The sharing economy is a viable alternative, as it can make many products and services more affordable. Furthermore, the sharing economy creates opportunities for market participants to generate additional income by sharing their assets or services. It is ironic that the sharing economy emerged shortly after the great financial recession of 2007–2008, claiming to change the world for better by providing a new pattern of consumption and work [10]. As the divide between the upper and middle classes is becoming larger, and the inflationary pressure is rising, the sharing economy can be considered very attractive. The sharing economy creates professional opportunities for many unemployed or under-employed workers. It can lead consumers to focus on utilization, rather than on ownership, and thus reduce unnecessary purchases. A major cause of the rise in sharing economy is its capacity in creating a symbiosis with the conventional economy. For instance, a large number of Uber's drivers work full time or part time in the conventional economy. In other words, the sharing economy can prosper not despite the conventional economy, but thanks to it. In comparison with many other businesses, the sharing economy startups require very little investment and hard assets. For instance, the accommodation giant Airbnb started modestly in a basement, and it still is operating with less than 600 employees.

Technological Drivers

The sharing economy is driven by the recent advancements in information technology that are able to match consumers and service providers. Big data, data analytics, social media, and mobile devices allow more efficiency. In the past decade, the payment systems have improved and allowed secure and prompt financial transactions among users. Thanks to the new technologies, the risks of fraud and error in the financial transactions have been hugely reduced [17].

The recent advances have created Internet Plus that encompasses a variety of high-technology applications in conventional industries. Internet Plus integrates all resources in a platform, activates the elements of sharing economy, offers the business models, and manages new credit systems [12].

Four Industries Revolutionized by the Sharing Economy

The sharing economy businesses offer both private and public resources such as merchandise, service, time, space, and capital surpluses. Some public resources are inherently shared, but the new technological platforms allow a more efficient allocation of such resources among multiple participants and across a larger geographic area [12]. For instance, municipalities, hospitals, libraries, sports facilities, and universities may share their unused or underused resources with remote areas. Currently, the sharing economy is revolutionizing four important sectors or industries: accommodation and hospitality, transportation and mobility, online labor market, and finance and lending.

Transport and Mobility

Transport and mobility are among the sectors that are undergoing significant transformations because of the advent of sharing economy. Two different types of platforms can be identified in the transportation sector. The first type allows the contracting of resources such as cars, motorbikes, and bicycles. Businesses such as ZipCar, EasyCar, Car2go, Autolib, and Velib belong to this first category. The second type allows users to rent vehicles together with labor. BlaBlaCar, Sidecar, Uber, and Lyft are famous examples of this second category. Car2go has more than one million members, is active in more than 29 cities across Europe and North America, and offers transportation on a by-the-minute basis. BlaBlaCar is a car-pooling service with more than 25 million members that allows drivers to share their empty seats with long-distance passengers. Uber is the most valuable business in the sharing economy that matches passengers and drivers [1]. In addition to car-sharing services, bike-share businesses like Bixi, Capital Bikeshare, and Citi Bike also are mushrooming across many metropolitan areas offering residents and tourists viable and convenient transport alternatives. As of 2013, bike-sharing businesses existed in more than 500 cities. Thanks to Internet Plus, users are now able to locate available bikes and open docks via mobile applications. Bike- and car-sharing businesses are expanding rapidly and are creating more convenient and sustainable transportation alternatives in urban centers [14].

These programs are becoming even more popular, as land values rise within metropolitan centers, and private car ownership becomes more expensive and less desirable. Private cars are idle for about 95 percent of the time, and even when they are driven, they are used often with an average of three to four empty seats [21]. The sharing businesses can have cars on the road and out of parking spaces for much of the day. This will result in a substantial reduction of the total number of cars to transport people. Consequently, the demand for parking spots in urban centers could decrease. The consumers can save on the cost of insurance, fuel, and repair [14]. Car- and bike-sharing businesses will change the face of big cities by reducing congestion, noise and air pollution. For example, parking spaces may be converted into public amenities such as parks, tennis courts, plazas, and farmer markets.

Accommodation and Hospitality

Accommodation and hospitality represent another attractive sector to the sharing economy businesses. Airbnb, HomeAway, HouseTrip, 9Flats, Wimdu, Onefinestay, Roomerama, Sleepout, Love Home Swap, and Holiday Lettings are some well-known platforms through which people can rent out properties or parts of properties. As the cost of housing is rising in many metropolitan areas, shared housing and cohousing are becoming more attractive. In a shared housing, couples or individuals combine their resources to rent and live in a home together. By contrast, in a cohousing, multiple households live in a community or multifamily structure. In the past decade, the millennials have been seeking these affordable options [14]. Banks are recognizing the impact of the sharing economy on lending and are considering appropriate measures. For example, a Credit Union in Canada has developed a product called a mixer mortgage, which allows multiple buyers to share a single mortgage [14]. The sharing economy has witnessed a raid and substantial growth in the short-term rental and accommodation industry. Some businesses like Airbnb, HomeAway, FlipKey, VRBO, and Roomorama have penetrated the hospitality industry through peer-to-peer rental services. The market of short-term rental is expected to grow significantly in the coming years, as it offers convenience and saving to travelers and additional income to the homeowners. Internet-based search engines, electronic payments, and mechanisms for peer review and ratings to ensure the quality have boosted the market expansion of short-term rentals.

Labor Market

The labor market is supposed to be massively affected by the sharing economy. Currently, there are many kinds of inefficiencies in labor markets. For instance, while many businesses are in a desperate need of qualified workers, almost 30 to 45 percent of the working-age population in countries around the world is unemployed, inactive, or working only part time [22]. The sharing economy platforms can rely on advanced technologies to connect individuals to the right work opportunities, and thus increase labor efficiency in many aspects. Many platforms are popping up that specialize in micro-tasking by matching employers and on-demand workers. Some examples in this category include Amazon Mechanical Tusk, Adtriboo, TaskRabbit, Oltretata, Freelancer, Crowdsource, Crowdflower, Clickworker, and Upwork [1]. Upwork is an online platform that connects workers who supply services with buyers who pay for and receive these services across the globe [23]. Using the Upwork platform, workers can contract with any firm directly. Upwork offers a complete management system by recording the time spent on the job, allowing communication between workers and employers, facilitating electronic monitoring. According to the McKinsey Global Institute, online platforms could add 2.7 trillion U.S. dollars, or 2.0 percent, to the global GDP and increase employment by 72 million full-time-equivalent positions by 2025 [22]. The sharing economy creates opportunities for job seekers to find jobs that suit their skills and preferences, offer transparency around the demand for skills, and allow students to make informed choices.

Finance and Lending

The rise of non-bank platforms such as Prosper, LendingClub, Kickstarter, Funding Circle, and Zopa implies that the sharing economy has gained popularity and acceptance in the money lending industry. The sharing economy businesses offer opportunities for financial transactions, which are being conducted between relevant parties without the intermediation of financial institutions [26]. The main advantage of sharing finance is that the lenders and borrowers can interact directly and do not have to pay fees to the banks and financial institutions. Therefore, lenders get fairly high returns, while borrowers benefit from low-cost loans. Like other business models of the sharing economy, the peer-to-peer lending networks represent convenience and efficiency for all market participants as they eliminate some of the difficulty and high costs associated with traditional lending, including advertising, overhead, and infrastructure expenses [5]. Such a collaborative finance is mainly beneficial to low-income borrowers, including students and young couples. While most of the activities are peer-to-peer lending, some platforms such as Kickstarter and IndieGogo match entrepreneurial projects with venture capitalists.

The Consequences of Sharing Economy

The sharing economy offers many opportunities for people to generate a full- or part-time employment and an additional source of income [27]. The flexibility of sharing business models enables people to earn extra income while doing their current occupations or education [29]. For example, many drivers work with Uber because of the flexibility it offers to earn money during their free hours [27]. Workers and suppliers benefit from a good degree of flexibility in choosing when to work or make their assets available, while users and consumers benefit from customized and on-demand services [28]. The sharing economy can moderate some of the consumerist tendencies in the industrialist countries where consumers see no problems with buying more and having more [29]. Furthermore, the sharing economy adopts different economic models, transforms the concept of work, and modernizes the labor market. Therefore, salary systems, social protection, and retirement plans that are historically linked to the conventional economy will have to change. Users of the sharing economy, both consumers and providers are empowered, so they can play an important role in forming the dynamism of markets. Reviews, ratings, and involvement can determine the reputation, prices, and by extension, the value of products and services [28]. As such, the sharing economy businesses have effective self-regulated mechanisms to control the quality of their services. The sharing economy brings about new challenges and disruptions. Most sharing businesses are unregulated and escape the government's scrutiny. As more business activities migrate to the sharing economy, the governments' revenues and taxation could decline, and public services may be disrupted. Sharing economy businesses may squeeze the conventional incumbents by offering lower prices and by tempting their customers.

Environmental Sustainability

The conventional economy is in interminable chase of higher production, consumption, and competition that necessarily put pressure on natural resources and pose various threats to the natural environment. Any efforts to protect the natural environment should focus on reducing consumption. It is impossible to tackle environmental problems such as greenhouse gas emissions, air pollution, global warming, water pollution, land degradation, and e-waste, without reducing the level of global consumption of goods, services, and commodities. The sharing economy focuses on smart utilization of resources, results in lower levels of consumption, and consequently improves environmental sustainability. According to the French Environment and Energy Management Agency, shareable goods account for about one-third of the household waste, implying that the sharing economy can have positive effects on the environment [28]. The most important feature of the sharing economy is its capacity to make the green and responsible consumption a natural component of business activities. Therefore, the goal of environmental protection is not imposed on the economy; rather it becomes part of it, and even serves wealth creation. Simply put, in the sharing economy, the environmental protection is achieved through business activity and not despite it.

Workers' Exploitation

While the sharing economy is supposed to rely on the spirit of collaboration and solidarity, a new critical perspective is increasingly gaining acceptance: the sharing economy brings about a new form of workers' exploitation. The proponents of this perspective argue that the sharing economy is destroying standard work arrangements and workers' protections under the pretext of technological innovation and efficiency [10]. They argue that business models such as Uber and Airbnb are damaging the bargaining power of workers because they have little control over the relations of production, benefits, and wages [30]. According to this view, in the sharing economy, the work relations are algorithmically determined, so it is extremely difficult for workers and regulators to understand how businesses operate [31]. As the supply of workers and providers increases, there will be more pressure on workers, and as a result, their work conditions will deteriorate. Furthermore, as most of the sharing economy business models consider workers as independent contractors, they have a good degree of freedom to define the wages, earnings, and work conditions and terminate the contracts. Some empirical studies on the sharing business models confirm that their workers are not generally well compensated, they are responsible for various expenses, and more importantly, they are deprived of benefits and the rights and protections guaranteed to standard employees [32]. Furthermore, the sharing economy workers are exposed to multiple risks, including physical perils and legal risks. What is particularly striking is that, when the sharing economy workers enter the contract out of necessity and as the principal job, the working conditions can be particularly painful and traumatic.

A Utopian View

According to some authors, notably Jeremy Rifkin, the sharing economy ushers us to a utopian society as the most essential goods and services will be produced with near-zero marginal cost [17]. With the advancement of the sharing economy, the free exchange of manufactured products will accelerate over time, the cost of production will decline, and ultimately, the concept of ownership will be eliminated or at least will be weakened. These transformations result in an abundant society where our material needs will be easily, and sometimes, freely satisfied. While this perspective seems naively optimistic, we suggest that the sharing economy may transform the idea of ownership, particularly with regard to some tangible assets such as vehicles and homes.

The Potential for Disruption

An important feature of every innovation, including the sharing economy, is its disruptive effects. According to Christensen [34], disruptive innovation can be described as "a process by which a product or service takes root initially in simple applications at the bottom of a market and then relentlessly moves up market, eventually displacing established competitors." A successful disruptive phenomenon does not happen suddenly, rather it grows gradually until it appears more attractive than the existing technologies or options when it becomes part of the mainstream. The sharing economy can bring about disruptions in traditional markets. For example, there are many complaints against unregulated or under-regulated business models such as Uber and Airbnb. People may rent their homes without complying with the existing regulations for hotel accommodation, or they may offer rides without complying with taxi regulations. There is a lack of checks and balances on drivers and vehicles. Workers' compensation is inadequate, and safety does not receive enough attention. Uber has tackled with governments and has experienced partial bans in many cities across the world, including Sydney, Amsterdam, Berlin, Paris, London, New York, San Francisco, and New Delhi.

New Risks

The sharing economy creates new problems and risks for low-income and vulnerable consumers and workers. The risks and problems of sharing businesses are particularly serious, as they often escape the control and scrutiny of the existing regulatory frameworks [35]. For instance, sharing economy businesses gain access to large amounts of users' sensitive information that could be used to their detriment in the future [36]. Furthermore, the sharing economy businesses may pose serious threats to the health and safety of their users, as most of them do not provide sufficient oversight and training because many of the service providers are not their full-time employees. Drivers, passengers, and on-demand workers may be threatened by dangerous, illegal, or unsafe tasks or situations [33]. For example, some Airbnb hosts have had their homes severely damaged and their relations with neighbors deteriorated [10]. Some Uber drivers have been accused of raping passengers or committing sexual assault. As trust is a key component of the sharing economy, lower-income people and visible minorities are at a disadvantage because they are seen as less trustworthy [5].

Benefits for Low-Income and Underserved Groups

The sharing economy models may have positive implications for low-income people and underserved groups by removing barriers of ownership and lowering the barriers to certain goods and services. For example, the lower income groups can benefit from a relatively easy access to cars and vacation homes. It is widely accepted that peer-to-peer platforms offer more inclusive and higher-quality consumption that might be achieved through traditional models [37]. Consumers may rent an entire apartment at the price of a mid-range priced hotel room or order a cab for half the price of a normal taxi fare [38]. Similarly, the sharing businesses can facilitate access to some basic services such as affordable meals, health care, and medical equipment [39]. Similarly, the sharing of business models may have positive effects on communities by strengthening local economies, standards of living, infrastructure, job creation, entrepreneurship, and social relations [7]. While the sharing economy has some benefits for low-income consumers, it is not assured whether these benefits can be sustainable in long term.

References

[1] Petropoulos, G. 2017. *An Economic Review of the Collaborative Economy* (No. 2017/5). Bruegel Policy Contribution.

[2] Owyang, J., A. Samuel, and A. Grenville. 2014. "Sharing is the New Buying: Vision Critical & Crowd, Companies." Available at https://visioncritical.com/resources/collaborative-economy-report/

[3] Martin, C.J. 2016. "The Sharing Economy: A Pathway to Sustainability or a Nightmarish form of Neoliberal Capitalism?" *Ecological Economics* 121, pp. 149–59.

[4] Goudin. 2016. *The Cost of Non-Europe in the Sharing Economy*. European Parliamentary Research Service, European Parliament.

[5] Economics, D.A. 2015. *The Sharing Economy and the Competition and Consumer Act*. September 20, 2015, http://accc. gov. au/publications

[6] Selloni, D. 2017. "New Forms of Economies: Sharing Economy, Collaborative Consumption, Peer-to-Peer Economy." In *CoDesign for Public-Interest Services*, 15–26. Springer, Cham.

[7] "An Inclusive Sharing Economy Unlocking Business Opportunities to Support Low-Income and Underserved Communities." 2016. https://bsr.org/reports/BSR_An_Inclusive_Sharing_Economy.pdf

[8] Taeihagh, A. 2017. "Crowdsourcing, Sharing Economies and Development." *Journal of Developing Societies* 33, no. 2, 191–222. doi:10.1177/0169796X17710072

[9] Dillahunt, T.R., and A.R. Malone. April 2015. "The Promise of the Sharing Economy Among Disadvantaged Communities." In *Proceedings of the 33rd Annual ACM Conference on Human Factors in Computing Systems*, 2285–94. ACM.

[10] Schor, J.B., and W. Attwood-Charles. 2017. "The 'Sharing' Economy: Labor, Inequality, and Social Connection on for-Profit Platforms." *Sociology Compass* 11, no. 8, p. e12493.

[11] Hamari, J., M. Sjöklint, and A. Ukkonen. 2015. "The Sharing Economy: Why People Participate in Collaborative Consumption." *Journal of the Association for Information Science and Technology*.

[12] China Council for International Cooperation on Environment and Development. 2016. "Sharing Economy: A New Economic Revolution Led by Lifestyles."

[13] Rifkin, J. 2011. *The Third Industrial Revolution: How Lateral Power is Transforming Energy, The Economy, and the World*. Macmillan.

[14] Madden, J. 2015. "Exploring the New Sharing Economy." *NAIOP Research Foundation. White Paper.* Retrieve from https://naiop.org/~/media/Research/Research/Research% 20Reports/Exploring% 20the% 20New, 20

[15] Pais, I., and G. Provasi. 2015. "Sharing Economy: A Step Toward the Re-Embeddedness of the Economy?" *Stato e Mercato* 35, no. 3, pp. 347–78.

[16] "All Eyes on the Sharing Economy." 2013. *The Economist.* March 9, http://economist.com/news/technology-quarterly/21572914-collaborative-consumption-technology-makes-it-easier-people-rent-items

[17] The Insurance Institute of Canada. 2017. Sharing Economy: Implications for the Insurance Industry in Canada.

[18] Botsman, R. 2015. "The Changing Rules of Trust in the Digital Age." *Harvard Business Review.* October 20, https://hbr.org/2015/10/the-changing-rules-of-trust-in-the-digital-age

[19] Consumer Intelligence Series. 2014. "The Sharing Economy." https://pwc.com/us/en/technology/publications/assets/pwc-consumer-intelligence-series-the-sharing-economy.pdf

[20] Reboot Illinois. 2016. "How the Sharing Economy Is Reshaping the Business Services Sector."2016. A Non-Partisan Organization Dedicated to Involving Illinois Residents in the State's Political Process.

[21] Coldewey, D. 2011. "Exploring Some Implications of Driverless Cars." *TechCrunch.* December 8, http://techcrunch.com/2011/12/08/googles-dutta-explores-some-implications-of-driverless-cars/

[22] Manyika, J., S. Lund, K. Robinson, J. Valentino, and R. Dobbs. 2015. "A Labor Market that Works: Connecting Talent with Opportunity in the Digital Age." *McKinsey Global Institute*, 20. http://mckinsey.com/~/media/McKinsey/dotcom/Insights/Employment%20and% 20growth/Connecting

[23] Horton, J., W.R. Kerr, and C. Stanton. 2017. *Digital Labor Markets and Global Talent Flows* (No. w23398). National Bureau of Economic Research.

[24] Recode.net, 2018. https://recode.net/2018/1/5/16854714/uber-four-billion-rides-coo-barney-harford-2018-cut-costs-customer-service

[25] https://press.airbnb.com/news/

[26] Mitręga-Niestrój, K. 2013. "The Sharing Economy and Collaborative Finance-Outline of the Problems." *Studia Ekonomiczne* 173, pp. 13–25.

[27] Hall, J., and A. Krueger. January 15, 2015. "An Analysis of the Labor Market for Uber's Driver-Partners in the United States." Retrieved April 12, 2016, from https://s3.amazonaws.com: https://s3.amazonaws.com/uber-static/comms/PDF/Uber_Driver-Partners_Hall_Kreuger_2015.pdf

[28] Ranjbari, M., G. Morales-Alonso, and R. Carrasco-Gallego. 2018. "Conceptualizing the Sharing Economy through Presenting a Comprehensive Framework." *Sustainability* 10, no. 7, p. 2336.

[29] van Welsum, D. 2016. "Sharing is Caring? Not Quite." *Some Observations About 'The Sharing Economy.'* World Development Report 2016—Digital Dividends (Background Paper102963). World Bank Group.

[30] Hill, S. 2015. *Raw Deal: How the "Uber Economy" and Runaway Capitalism Are Screwing American Workers.* St. Martin's Press.

[31] Scholz, T. 2017. *Uberworked and Underpaid: How Workers are Disrupting the Digital Economy.* John Wiley & Sons.

[32] Bernhardt, A. 2014. *Labor Standards and the Reorganization of Work: Gaps in Data and Research.*

[33] Ravenelle, A. 2015. *A Return to Gemeinschaft: Digital Impression Management and the Sharing Economy.* Unpublished paper, City University of New York.

[34] Christensen, C. 2016. "Disruptive Innovation." *Key Concepts.* http://claytonchristensen.com/key-concepts/

[35] Kamenetz, A. 2013. "Does the Sharing Economy Have a Shadow Side." *Fast Company* [Online]. Available at http://fastcompany.com/3013272/does-the-sharing-economy-have-a-shadowside (accessed April 1, 2015).

[36] Ramasastry, A. 2015. "Too Much Sharing in the Sharing Economy? Uber's Use of Our Passenger Data Highlights the Perils of Data Collection via Geolocation." *Verdict.* https://verdict.justia.com/2015/02/10/much-sharing-sharing-economy

[37] Fraiberger, S.P., and A. Sundararajan. 2015. "Peer-to-Peer Rental Markets in the Sharing Economy." NYU Stern School of Business Research Paper. http://ssrn.com/abstract=2574337

[38] Ehrenfreund, M. 2015. "Where the Poor and Rich Really Spend Their Money." *Washington Post.* https://washingtonpost.com/news/wonk/wp/2015/04/14/where-the-poor-and-rich-spend-really-spend-their-money/

[39] Ehrenfreund, M. 2015. "Where the Poor and Rich Really Spend Their Money." *Washington Post.* https://washingtonpost.com/news/wonk/wp/2015/04/14/where-the-poor-and-rich-spend-really-spend-their-money/

CHAPTER 5

The Fourth Industrial Revolution

1. The Making of the Fourth Industrial Revolution
2. The Implications of the Fourth Industrial Revolution
3. The Industrial Internet
4. Managing the Fourth Industrial Revolution

The Making of the Fourth Industrial Revolution

According to Klaus Schwab [1], we are currently witnessing the emergence of an all-inclusive revolution that is going to essentially change the way we live, work, and relate to one another [2]. Schwab popularized the term *Forth Industrial Revolution* (4IR) to refer to the confluence of mainly technological innovations, including artificial intelligence (AI) robotics, nanotechnology, biotechnology, quantum computing, blockchain, Internet of Things, and 3D printing. Schwab suggests that the 4IR is expected to affect all aspects of our lives "unlike anything humankind has ever experienced" [3]. Schwab [3] maintains that the world has witnessed four industrial revolutions: the First Industrial Revolution allowed the use of steam engines for mechanical production and happened around 1784 or almost 235 years ago. The introduction of the factory system, the development of the railroad, and huge advances in metallurgy and chemistry are some consequences of the First Industrial Revolution [4]. The Second Industrial Revolution happened at the beginning of the 20th century and relied on electricity, mass production, and the division of labor. The Second Industrial Revolution resulted in the development of electricity networks, telephone lines, automobiles, gas turbines, artificial fertilizer, and similar technologies that transformed transport, communication, and consumption [4]. The Third Industrial Revolution took place in the late 1970s and matured sometime around the early 2000s. The Third Industrial Revolution relied mainly on the advances in information technology, production of the integrated circuits, microprocessors, and digital telecommunications. All these technologies were integrated into the Internet and mobile telephony and completely changed our lives. Currently, we are at the early stages of the 4IR, which is marked by increasing reliance on cyber–physical systems as the basis of intelligent network systems and processes. The 4IR is ushering us to a digital transformation that universally influences all aspects of human civilizations across the globe including, work, energy, production, governance, education, and recreation. In the 4IR, technologies amplify each other across the physical, digital, and biological spheres and revolutionize our lives by disrupting the conventional industries, thus creating new business models, and reformatting production, consumption, transportation, and delivery systems [5]. Hence, the 4IR is not about particular innovative technologies, it is rather about their complex and wide-ranging confluence. The 4IR is a paradigm shift that affects how we produce, how we consume, and how we work, but it goes beyond the economic and business boundaries. The 4IR is unlike anything humankind has experienced in the past. At this time, new businesses are developed based on their capacity to link the physical and virtual worlds. In a near future, by infusion of multiple technologies and transformation, the conventional boundaries of the physical, digital, and biological worlds will be broken.

We may identify three major characteristics of the 4IR as high velocity, systematic impact, and zero marginal cost. First, the 4IR is marked by its high velocity because it is mounting at an exponential, rather than a linear pace, breath, and depth. It took almost 120 years for the First Industrial Revolution to spread outside the European continent, but took only less than a decade for the Internet to pervade across the globe. In the case of the 4IR, we may expect drastic changes across the globe in a few years. More and more, we are living in an accelerated and interconnected world, so each powerful technology generates technologies that are even faster and more powerful. The second characteristic of the 4IR is its systematic impact. While the previous industrial revolutions initially influenced particular aspects of the human economy in certain countries, the 4IR involves the transformation of entire systems across and within societies, markets, industries, and the whole planet. Third, the 4IR bridges the gap between virtual and physical spheres on both production and consumption sides and leads to the zero marginal costs. Many businesses and consumers will produce and consume informational goods that imply zero cost of storage, transportation, and replication [4].

The main pillars of the 4IR are cyber–physical systems, intelligent data gathering, and data storage and distribution systems [1]. The new digital technologies such as blockchain will revolutionize the collaboration and engagement of organizations, workers, and consumers. Developments in information technologies, combined with robotization, automation of tasks, Internet of Things, advanced manufacturing, driverless cars, cyber weapons, sensors, biotechnology, and surveillance, will fuel the economic growth and wealth creation [6]. The electronic devices will become an inevitable part of consumers' lives, as they can anticipate the consumers' needs. Due to the availability of data, production and consumption will be highly precise, and the amount of waste will decrease substantially [1]. The main beneficiaries of the 4IR are the providers of intellectual capital, innovators, and shareholders of new business entities. Consequently, the gap in wealth and power between the workers and capitalists may deepen even more [1]. To deal with speed and impacts of the 4IR, the businesses have to stay agile and competitive by offering innovative products and services. Indeed, in the 4IR, the competitiveness of businesses will depend much more on their innovative capacity than on their cost-effectiveness. Established companies will constantly come under extreme pressure by emerging disruptors and innovators from other industries and countries [1].

The Implications of the Fourth Industrial Revolution

Implications for Businesses

The most important implications of new technologies so far have been related to the consumption experience. In recent years, consumers around the world have greatly benefited from lower prices, abundance of products, and associated improved quality of life. With the advent of the 4IR, there will be significant transformations in the supply side and long-term achievements in productivity. Consequently, transportation, communication, trade, logistics, and global supply chains costs will decline drastically

[1]. While the cost of doing business tends to decline in the future, the economic inequality is expected to rise because labor markets may be disrupted, and automation could sweep across the global economy. It is too difficult to predict the implications of the new economic setting on the labor, but consistent with the existing trends, the importance of talent as a critical factor of production will continue to grow. Consequently, the job market may be divided into two opposite poles as low-skill or low-pay versus high-skill or high-pay [1]. This cleavage in the workforce, and thus in income, could lead to greater levels of economic inequality across the world. The income inequality might be transformed into a winner-takes-all economy that offers only limited opportunities to the majority of the population. Due to its peculiar nature, the main winners of the 4IR are expected to be the providers of intellectual and physical capital, including the innovators, shareholders, and investors. In the evolving economic system, there will be more demand for educated and highly skilled workers. The ordinary workers will be surprised by the extent of stagnation of their income levels over the course of the next few years.

The existing value chains in many industries will be disrupted by a combination of technological and competitive factors. The agile and innovative competitors who have access to global digital platforms may beat the conventional incumbents by improving the quality, speed, and price [1]. Similarly, the demand and consumption behavior are expected to undergo major transformations, as new technologies will result in more transparency and consumer interaction. As a result, many businesses will have to customize not only their products and services, but also their marketing campaigns. The advances of smart platforms will be matching the supply and demand so efficiently that the conventional business structures could be extremely disrupted [1]. Therefore, it is possible to suggest that the 4IR may have major business effects on customer expectations, product enhancement, collaborative innovation, and organizational forms. According to Schwab, the Third Industrial Revolution was focusing on digitization, but the 4IR offers a complex confluence of multiple technologies in all industries [1]. The 4IR will enable businesses to exploit the interaction of digital, physical, and human realms and create economic value by offering services, rather than products.

The Second Industrial Revolution popularized the hierarchical organizational structure, unity of command, and strict managerial controls.

By contrast, the competitiveness of the organization in the era of the 4IR will depend increasingly on the extent of their organizational flexibility. Organizations will move from hierarchical and centralized structures to more networked and collective models [1]. Such flexible structures will help organizations deal with the uncertainty and disruption of emerging technological transformations.

Implications for Governments

The existing systems of public administration have been built around the social structure of the Second Industrial Revolution with centralized, linear, and rigid decision-making organizations in which the administrators and policymakers could take time to study, deliberate, and develop the appropriate regulations. With the advent of the 4IR, the socio-technological innovations will push the governments to change their traditional administration systems by adopting less centralized and more open approaches to policymaking. The adaptation of public administration will necessitate more agility, innovation, and collaboration with the private sector, businesses, and civil society. Those governments that cannot adapt their structures to these new trends may experience disruption and dysfunctionality. Because of the 4IR, the demarcation between physical and digital spaces will continue to erode, and new hybrid interfaces will be created. Under these circumstances, state power will be shared with non-state actors, and its institutional influence will be shared with nebulous networks. The citizens will be able to express their opinions, get involved in governments, and direct their collective efforts. At the same time, the confluence of physical and digital spaces will enable governments to increase their control over populations, monitor their activities, and track their movements. The 4IR may have serious consequences for national security, as new technologies and the confluence of virtual and physical spaces will result in the occurrence of cyber-attacks, and hybrid and asymmetrical confrontation. The modern conflicts will be less conventional and more complex than ever. This implies that the demarcation between war and peace will be more blurry, and future conflicts could involve the widespread use of autonomous and sophisticated weaponry.

Implications for Citizens

The 4IR is expected to affect many aspects of our lives including the perceptions of communication, socialization, consumption, ownership, leisure, and time. The integration of new technologies into our lives will result in human augmentation that may drastically change our identity as human beings [1]. The integration of technology into human lives could deprive them of many essential human capacities such as emotion, conversation, interaction, and reflection. For example, the technological innovations in biotechnology and AI may change the essential human characteristics associated with health, cognition, and emotions.

The Second Industrial Revolution and the division of work created long-lasting patterns in our collective psyche, including the linear perception of time, protection of privacy, and commitment to one task at a time. With the advent of the 4IR, temporal circularity shared privacy, and increasing levels of multitasking will replace these behavioral and cultural traits. In the 4IR, customers are at the focus of the digital economy, as the new technologies will enable businesses to serve their customers more effectively. Customers can be identified based on their previous experience. Thanks to further advances in data analytics, customer service is expected to become even more personalized and faster than ever [11].

The conventional education system is deeply rooted in the Second Industrial Revolution and even in the European traditions of the middle ages. It is marked by a slow pace of change, distinct disciplines, formal lectures, structured programs, and devotion to some particular professions. The ultimate goal of many schools is still to train ideal employees. Education is expected to become more student-oriented and technologically intensive to keep up with the major business and technological transformations of the 4IR. This will necessitate new skills and qualifications for teachers and faster adaptation to the world of work [7].

The Industrial Internet

The digitization of the economy means that many tasks in our life can be reduced to a few sequences of the human-to-machine,

machine-to-machine, and machine-to-human chains. The digital technologies are creating new combinations of mental, physical, and mechanical work. The integration of information technology and operational technology in many industries will lead to cost reduction, improved quality, and efficiency [1]. According to Siegfried Dasch from Bosch [1], in future manufacturing, everything will be linked to everything else so that the virtual–real processes will improve productivity. In other words, the future of manufacturing will be an interplay between the real and digital. General Electric has used the term *Industrial Internet* to refer to the addition of digital technology to all machines and all devices. For instance, General Electric is adding sensors in the engines of planes, trains, and MRI scanners to make aviation, railway services, and healthcare, respectively, more efficient. According to the General Electric's estimates, the Industrial Internet could save the aviation sector two billion U.S. dollars a year [1]. This kind of smart manufacturing can be used in many industries from food to consumer goods and the high-tech sector. The addition of networked software to products and machines will enable businesses to gain in several areas. For example, by enabling machine-to-machine communication without human intervention, the need for human work is reduced, and important contributions to efficiency and security are made. Machine-to-machine applications rely on microelectronics and wireless technology to gather and distribute real-time data in a network. For example, the Parker Water and Sanitation District in Colorado is linking pumps and pipes in the systems via a software-controlled water system to optimize the use of mechanical, human, and natural sources [1]. Businesses can use the Industrial Internet to conveniently conduct their upgrades and maintenance tasks and improve the reliability and speed of their operations. The Internet of Things will be used to interact with customers in real time via all kinds of domestic appliances such as refrigerators, toothbrushes, televisions, and vacuum cleaners. The users' data can be collected in order to create business value and to offer services more efficiently. According to the Cisco estimates, the total market value of the Internet of Things will be worth 14 trillion U.S. dollars in 2022 [1]. Most of the Internet of Things market will be dedicated to manufacturing that will be valued about 3.88 trillion U.S. dollars.

Managing the Fourth Industrial Revolution

Most of the industrial countries have experienced a steady and significant rate of economic growth (gross domestic product per capita) since the First Industrial Revolution in the 1800s. Before the First Industrial Revolution, much of Europe was suffering from low or zero economic growth accompanied by social stagnation [8]. After the First Industrial Revolution, new technologies combined with mechanization, automation, and specialization stimulated the Western European economies and resulted in the creation of unprecedented wealth and higher standards of living [9]. For instance, real income per person in the Organization for Economic Co-operation and Development (OECD) economies has risen almost 2,900 percent since 1800 [10]. According to the World Economic Forum [4], in the recent decades, many advanced economies are showing signs of decline as they are failing to preserve the rate of economic growth and living standards for their citizens [11].

As the world is entering the 4IR, the introduction of emerging technologies is expected to alter the relationships and power dynamics between governments, companies, communities, and citizens. It is plausible to believe that, in the new era, economic crises will be no longer linear, rather they will occur simultaneously, side by side, and due to their velocity, will not leave us enough time to react, contemplate, plan, and strategize. Indeed, emerging crises will be various in nature; they will range from geopolitical, ecological, and political, to technological, financial, and economic factors. Due to much uncertainty and ambiguity surrounding the 4IR, many observers remain cautious and even pessimistic about the future socio-economic conditions. The growing power of tech giants and the subsequent concerns such as the elimination of jobs, loss of privacy, transformation of identity, and dominance of AI are some scary outcomes associated with the 4IR [12]. The 4IR can eliminate not only the low-wage and low-skilled jobs, but also those jobs that bring prodigious benefits. Furthermore, the 4IR may aggravate a harmful cleavage, which already exists in the distribution of wealth. A small number of talented people take on the majority of complex tasks, and a large number of citizens lose their jobs and remain unemployed or underemployed.

In the past three decades, many developing countries have taken advantage of the global business environment to achieve rapid rates of economic growth. Some emerging economies, notably China, have adopted technological sophistication and reached higher standards of living and productivity. Similarly, some developing countries benefited from this environment and achieved rapid rates of economic growth and poverty reduction. Consequently, the world as a whole has enriched, and the number of the abject poor has fallen significantly, but the advanced economies of the West have grown much more slowly [13]. The Third Industrial Revolution has resulted in lower labor and capital costs and easier access to global markets. At the same time, many countries, notably the developed Western economies, have experienced economic pressure from dislocation, skills mismatches, long-term unemployment, and wage stagnation. The rising levels of income inequality and prospects of growth preoccupy many developed economies. Consequently, there is a mounting pressure on social and political institutions to find solutions. By promising quick fixes, the right-wing parties, demagogues, and populist politicians are gaining popularity in the Western nations from Europe to North America. Currently, there are major concerns about emerging technologies among populations. These concerns are related to the impacts of new technologies on employment, security, privacy, food, and income inequality, among others [8]. Many advanced countries are incapable of upholding the rate of increase in living standards for their citizens. For instance, over the course of the past five years, annual median incomes have declined by 2.4 percent in the OECD economies, while the wage gaps have increased [14].

With all its radical transformations, the 4IR is expected to exacerbate the existing socio-economic drifts, threatening large segments of both developed and emerging countries [4]. While the waves of the 4IR could destroy the structure of the current economies, the ensuing innovative technologies and business models could generate exciting opportunities for improving employment, productivity, and quality of life. The 4IR may result in new levels of affluence as an enhanced quality of life, shorter working days, and increased family time [14]. The technologies such as machine learning, AI, and automated vehicles could significantly enhance the quality of life of citizens. The 4IR relies on the idea that a confluence of technological systems should serve human beings in sustainable and inclusive ways [4]. To deal with the adverse effects of the 4IR, a new human-centered economic model is required, in which the emphasis is put on social inclusion, wealth distribution, and social justice. Considering the paradigmatic shifts of the 4IR, the policymakers should rely on a more wide-ranging approach by prioritizing their citizens and their welfare instead of stimulating the short-term economic growth. In preparation for the 4IR, first, policymakers should take adequate measures to address the problems caused by the Third Industrial Revolution and globalization. Then, they should plan to capitalize on the opportunities and technologies of the 4IR. The G20 countries have highlighted three main strategies to deal with the challenges of the 4IR: management of aggregate demand through macroeconomic policy, export-led growth through trade and industrial policy, and regional integration combined with domestic deregulation [14]. Facing the enormous challenges of the 4IR, the governments should reinstate their confidence in the capacity of the liberal political and economic order to embrace new technologies and achieve a comprehensive and sustainable growth.

References

[1]   Schwab, K. 2017. *The Fourth Industrial Revolution*. Crown Business.

[2]   Bloem, J., M. Van Doorn, S. Duivestein, D. Excoffier, R. Maas, and E. Van Ommeren. 2014. *The Fourth Industrial Revolution*. Things Tighten.

[3]   Effoduh, J.O. 2016. "The Fourth Industrial Revolution by Klaus Schwab." *The Transnational Human Rights Review* 3. http://digitalcommons.osgoode. yorku.ca/thr/vol3/iss1/4

[4]   Samans, R., and N. Davis. 2017. "Advancing Human-Centred Economic Progress in the Fourth Industrial Revolution." *Recuperado de*, http://www3. weforum.org/docs/WEF_Advancing_Human-Centred_Economic_ Progress_WP_2017. pdf

[5]   Bloem, J., M. Van Doorn, S. Duivestein, D. Excoffier, R. Maas, and E. Van Ommeren. 2014. *The Fourth Industrial Revolution*. Things Tighten.

[6]   McKenzie, F. 2017. *The Fourth Industrial Revolution and International Migration*.

[7]   "Lisbon International Trade Fair, Learning, Working, and Competing in the Horizon of the 4th Industrial Revolution." 2017. *Social Dialogue on the Emergence of the Fourth Industrial Revolution: Education, Employment*

and Youth, 30–31, March | Lisbon Futurália–http://medsocialdialogue.org/sites/default/files/A_1.2.3_Report_SOLID.pdf

[8] Historical Data on Economic Activity Prior to 1800 are Patchy but Have Benefitted from Innovative Work by a Range of Scholars. See, for example, Fouquet, R., and S.N. Broadberry. 2015. "Seven Centuries of European Economic Growth and Decline." In *Journal of Economic Perspectives* 29, no. 4, Available at http://lse.ac.uk/ GranthamInstitute/wp-content/uploads/2015/09/Working- Paper-206-Fouquet-and-Broadberry.pdf

[9] "The Maddison Project Database Indicates that Average Yearly Per Capita Growth in the United Kingdom Rose from 0.1% Between 1400–1700 to 0.3% from 1700–1800, to 0.7% from 1800–1900 and 1.6% from 1900–2000." 2013. Available at http://ggdc.net/maddison/maddison-project/data.htm, 2013 version

[10] McCloskey, D.N. 2016. *Bourgeois Equality*. University of Chicago Press.

[11] Centers for Disease Control and Prevention analysis for the United States, which found life expectancy for the US population in 2015 was 78.8 years, a decrease of 0.1 year from 2014. CDC. "Mortality in the United States, 2015." December 2016. Available at https://cdc.gov/nchs/products/databriefs/db267.htm

[12] Briscoe, D., I. Tarique, and R. Schuler. 2012. *International Human Resource Management: Policies and Practices for Multinational Enterprises*. Routledge.

[13] "G20 Enhanced Structural Reform Agenda." September 2016. *Prepared by the G20 Framework Working Group*, Available at http://mofa.go.jp/files/000185875.pdf

[14] Samans, R., and N. Davis. 2017. "Advancing Human-Centred Economic Progress in the Fourth Industrial Revolution." *Recuperado de*. http://www3.weforum.org/docs/WEF_Advancing_Human-Centred_Economic_Progress_WP_2017.pdf

CHAPTER 6

The Gig Economy

The Rise of the Gig Economy

The gig economy is a popular term referring to various forms of work and employment marked by short-term, on-demand, and unpredictable arrangements. The gig economy is above all a technology-influenced development of labor that is transforming the conventional norms and beliefs about the place of work in society and the respective responsibilities of workers, businesses, and governments [1]. In the gig economy, workers no longer choose between working either as an employee or as a business owner. They may take a third path. While they are not subject to the restrictions and control of their employer, they do not have to start and run their own businesses. By using mobile applications, gig workers can tap into the existing infrastructure and customer network of an online platform company while maintaining the freedom of setting their own hours and choosing which jobs to take [2]. In contrast to a typical business owner, the average gig workers are generally younger and less financially sophisticated and tend to work fewer hours and make less money [3].

The gig-economy may include two forms of work: crowdwork and work on-demand [4]. Crowdwork is about completing some tasks through online platforms that put in contact an indefinite number of organizations and individuals [5]. By contrast, work on-demand implies the execution of some activities such as transport, cleaning, and clerical work via applications managed by firms that also intervene in setting the minimum quality standards of service and in the selection and management of the workforce [6]. Both types of gig work rely on the Internet and new technologies to match demand and supply of work and services at an extremely high speed. Because of their reliance on advanced technologies, both types of gig work are highly efficient, minimize transaction costs, and streamline frictions on markets [7]. By relying on digital platforms, freelancers may quickly connect with customers or employers to offer their products, services, or skills and secure payments. Very often, the gig work is a means of generating additional income outside of regular employment or a full-time job [8]. A gig worker can be defined as an independent contractor who freely contracts via an app or web-based platform [1]. In a gig economy, the term employer refers to those who are responsible to pay the gig worker directly or indirectly. Under such circumstances, it is difficult to distinguish between employees of a company and its contractors or service providers. Consequently, the demarcation between employment and entrepreneurship becomes so blurred that the two terms may be considered as interchangeable. Indeed, the term employer could be misleading in a gig economy because the so-called employer does not hire gig workers. For instance, in the case of Uber and many other electronic platforms, the riders and beneficiaries hire the driver, and the platforms simply connect them and manage payments [1]. While the platforms like Uber do not hire drivers, they are fully involved in the processes, as they are responsible for providing services and equipment, making decisions, setting the rates, and activating or deactivating drivers.

While much of the debate about the gig economy and alternative employment has focused on the sharing economy platforms such as Uber and Airbnb, it is important to mention that such platforms account for only a small share of the gig workers [12]. According to the Freelancers Union, there are almost 54 million independent workers comprising 34 percent of workers [13]. Of course, many of these independent workers may have more than one job, and depending on their employment, can be categorized as an employee or independent contractor. The number of gig workers who rely only on digital platforms is estimated around 600,000, of which 400,000 work for Uber [14]. By any measure, we can say that the number of gig workers is already huge and is rapidly rising.

This quick rise in the number and share of gig workers is transforming the American economy. It is widely expected that the economy of tomorrow will not consist of employments, but rather gigs. People will not have an employer, rather they will perform tasks, coordinated through faceless online platforms and compensated through digital transfers [15].

We are in the midst of a fundamental shift in the U.S. economy. Only a few decades ago, the average worker could remain with the same employer and job for the total duration of their career. The employees used to profit from a wide range of benefits, including job security, unemployment insurance, and retirement plans. Things have changed, as conventional employment is not the norm anymore, and a growing number of people work autonomously and combine income from multiple sources [16]. According to the Federal Reserve, the share of workers earning income from multiple jobs increased from 15 percent to 22 percent between 2014 and 2015 [17]. Similarly, Katz and Krueger [18] report that there was an increase of 9.4 million workers in alternative work arrangements in the past decade.

Some surveys and estimates show that most of the employment growth in the U.S. economy from 2005 to 2015 is attributed to the gig workers [9]. Based on a recent survey, currently, there are 3.2 million gig workers, growing at an 18.5 percent to reach 7.6 million by 2020 [10]. Despite the occurrence of the global financial crisis, gig workers in the United States grew at a rapid pace between 8.8 percent and 14.4 percent from 2002 to 2014 [11]. Self-employed and on-demand workers are expected to exceed 40 percent of the American workforce by 2020 [19]. These transformations have been happening for many years, and the nature of work is changing drastically.

Context of the Gig Economy

The Motivations

Flexibility is recognized as the main reason why people prefer gig work. Above all, workers appreciate the fact that they can choose their work environment and their work schedule [9]. The youth are particularly interested in autonomous and flexible employment. In recent years, an increasing number of workers are using new information technologies to carry out their tasks remotely. Some studies indicate that, because of such flexibility, most of the gig workers have shown higher levels of engagement and satisfaction with their work [20]. For instance, according to one recent study, more than 80 percent of the independent contractors and freelance workers indicated their preference for flexible work arrangement to being an employee [9]. Interestingly, gig workers may prefer flexibility to benefits in a usual schedule. For example, another recent study revealed that 55 percent of the Australians would take a 20 percent salary cut in order to work from home [11].

After the great financial crisis of 2007–2008, unemployment rates surged, and in the post-Great Recession era, the unemployment for many years stayed high. The increasing difficulty in finding decent employment opportunities led many job seekers to the gig work [21]. Another motivation behind the rise of gig work resides in a growing financial disparity in America and the stagnating wage levels over the course of the past three decades. Since the 1970s, American purchasing power, as a whole, has been stagnant, and low-income workers have experienced more financial hardship. This increasing financial pressure has led many to seek additional income in the gig economy. It is estimated that more than 31 percent of Uber drivers have sought additional income in undertaking a gig work [22].

Another important driver of the gig economy is the value creation in businesses and their commitment to shareholders. In the past decade, many businesses have relied on optimization of their workforce to increase productivity and profitability. Accordingly, the gig workers are on-demand personnel who can create value without the cost and inconvenience of permanency, bonuses, and benefits [23]. Conventional employees can be much more expensive than on-demand contractors or contingent workers. Federal and state unemployment taxes, social security and Medicare, pensions, health insurance, training, and workers' compensation premiums are examples of costs associated with conventional employment. Furthermore, employers may face other hurdles such as employment regulations, minimum wage requirements, and collective bargaining [1].

One major driver of the gig economy is the efficiency of the labor market that is done mainly via electronic platforms. On the one hand, online platforms connect workers and employers and enable them to efficiently exchange work and compensation. On the other hand, the gig economy enables businesses to find the right specialization and economies of scale of contractors [24]. Moreover, the gig economy enables businesses to scale according to demand, so they will be able to search, interview, hire, and terminate their contractors more effectively [25].

The Profile of Gig Workers

Gig workers are diverse; they come in all ages, education levels, incomes brackets, occupations, and nationalities. The gig economy is an emerging trend associated with advanced technologies, and naturally, it remains popular among the younger generations. At the global level, between 46 and 60 percent of the young people participate in the gig economy. The youth account for a quarter of gig workers [26]. Other age groups show significant interest in the gig economy as well. Women make up around 50 percent of the gig workforce. While age and gender are not issues in the gig economy, it seems that the household income level has some important effects on the degree of participation in the gig economy. It is found that people from low-income groups are more likely to partic- ipate in the gig workforce [26]. Gig workers are found in a wide range of industries from construction trades, household and personal services, and transportation, to professional services such as accounting, interior design, and writing and editing. According to the McKinsey Global Institute, those gig workers with lower levels of education and skills are more likely to work out of necessity [26]. Therefore, we can categorize gig workers as primary or supplemental earners depending on whether they work by choice or out of economic necessity [27]. A large number of gig workers choose this working style because they value its indepen- dence and flexibility. Many gig workers choose their work as a matter of preference, not a necessity [26]. Generally, gig workers are more involved in their tasks, show more interest in what they do, and enjoy the freedom and flexibility of their job. Therefore, in comparison with conventional workers, gig workers seem more satisfied with their occupations and are happier with their overall level of income. Even those working out of obli- gation typically appreciate the flexibility of the gig work. Even with regard to income security and benefits, it seems that gig workers are as satisfied as traditional workers are [27].

The Rise of the Gig Economy in Developing Countries

Gig economy and on-demand platforms are becoming gradually dominant across the world, particularly in developing countries, because of the rapid growth in digital connectivity [28]. According to the International Telecommunications Union (ITU), in 2016, there were about 898 million more Internet users than in 2013 [29]. It is estimated that, currently, around 48 percent of the global population is using the Internet. The number of people subscribed to mobile services is constantly increasing in Africa, particularly in countries such as Egypt, Nigeria, and South Africa. The substantial increase in the Internet connectivity predicts the promising future of the gig economy in developing countries. In many developing countries, unemployment and poor working conditions may offer incentives for workers to switch from formal employment to the on-demand economy [29]. The growth of middle-income earners with significant disposable incomes is another driver of the gig economy in developing countries [30]. On-demand platforms devoted to serving domestic workers are evolving in many developing countries such as India, Mexico, and South Africa. While the share of such services is still negligible, the recent studies suggest promising growth potentials [31].

The Dark Side of the Gig Economy

The gig work is part of a larger trend toward the casualization of labor in modern economies. Consistent with this trend, corporations are seeking more efficiency and less commitment to managing their human resources. They are developing work arrangements such as zero-hour contracts and on-call labor that bring about the possibility to hire-and-fire a significant portion of the workforce on an on-demand basis [32].

The gig economy creates numerous opportunities for workers, but it attracts a large number of contractors and gradually creates more competition among independent workers. Like any other labor market, the average income of gig workers is determined by the makeup of the pool of workers. Consequently, the increased competition among independent workers necessarily reduces workers' income levels, worsens work conditions, and raises the likelihood of their joblessness. Due to the high levels of flexibility, the gig workers are more likely to change their jobs, fill the vacant positions, or compete with the conventional workers or their gig counterparts. Therefore, the level of competition in a gig labor market tends to be even higher than that of a conventional economy. What makes the gig workers very vulnerable is that the technological advancement of digital platforms and their rising popularity are expected to increase the level of pressure on them.

Another major concern for gig workers is their vulnerability to the abuse of large corporations because they are not protected by state and federal regulations such as minimum wage requirements or unemployment insurance, workers' compensation, and disability insurance [1]. It is widely known that gig workers do not have access to sick pay, maternity pay, holiday pay, employer pension contributions, and many other benefits of employees. Furthermore, gig workers face many difficulties like reduced access to credit, the risk of not being paid for work that is already performed, complex tax filings, licensing, and regulatory compliance requirements [26]. In general, a full-time employee with regular and steady paycheck has better access to home financing and credit than a gig worker does. Gig workers often face financial instability, as they do not have access to steady employment income, they do not save enough for their retirement and do not benefit from health and disability insurance [33]. In some cases, gig workers face abuse or non-payment of clients and may suffer from substantial financial loses. Another concern is that gig workers often suffer from higher levels of risk associated with their tasks and are not subject to strict safety regulations. They often remain unprotected and unsupported against the work-related hazards. In the absence of effective regulation, gig workers are subject to discrimination from clients and colleagues. The flexibility of gig work remains very attractive to both workers and organizations, but this flexibility should not be considered as an absolute advantage. Indeed, the flexibility of gig work may not be necessary for a large portion of workers and could reduce the competence of some professions [34]. The rise of the gig work is a potentially disruptive phenomenon [36]. For instance, it is not clear that existing federal and state tax regulations can be applied to gig workers. In many cases, the rationale behind the formation of gig work is the evasion of conventional regulations, including tax codes [15].

Due to the confusion regarding the definition of employment, there are many cases of litigation over worker misclassification lawsuits in various U.S. jurisdictions. Some argue that, to resolve these issues; a hybrid category of employment should be created positioned between n employee and independent contractor [35]. The proponents of the third category argue that the novelty of the gig work causes social and organizational transformations, and thus requires novel treatment and regulation [35]. Indeed, the Internet platforms and customers could not be considered employers [35]. Therefore, instead of litigating the issue of whether a particular worker merits employee status, gig workers may be put under a different umbrella.

Implications of the Gig Economy for Businesses

The gig economy increases the fluidity of the workforce, and consequently impacts on organizations' structure and their hiring systems. Businesses in general view non-traditional staffing as a vital facet of their overall corporate strategy that provides fresh and various skills [37]. The main beneficiaries of the gig workers are those businesses that take advantage of fluid human capital to scale up and down on a project basis [38]. For example, it takes on average 2.7 days to hire a freelancer in contrast to more than 34 days to hire a conventional full-time worker [39]. The promptness and flexibility of companies in hiring and dismissing the gig workers mean that they can quickly start additional projects without significant investment and preparation [39]. Furthermore, the global reach of new technologies means that businesses have access to the best reservoir of talent around the world. The globalization of contingent workers has opened the door to a broader pool of talented and hardworking professionals at competitive rates [40]. Incorporating freelancers into the conventional workforce is seen as a smart move that often causes higher levels of productivity [41]. The gig economy could be particularly beneficial to small and medium businesses, as they are marked by serious limitations in their financial, technological, and human resources and do not afford to hire and retain full-time talented employees. The gig work allows many corporations to keep core operations focused on what they do best and call in independent service providers on demand. Because of this flexibility, they can add new capabilities without disrupting their regular operations. [26]. The gig economy is structured around networks, rather than traditional institutions [43], and because of its flexibility, can disrupt the conventional societal and organizational norms. In the gig economy, organizations and businesses rely on provisional and independent con-tractors to operate efficiently and deliver their on-demand services [44]. The flexible management of workers enables organizations to utilize the commercial value in underused personal assets according to the demand conditions [45]. In other words, the gig economy applies the notion of just-in-time management to the workforce to attain at the lowest levels of cost and the highest levels of profitability. For that reason, companies in the gig economy do not have to spend money on benefits, training, and development of their personnel [46].

As businesses increasingly rely on freelancers, they have to develop systems to manage them effectively. Indeed, gig workers are highly move-able and can easily switch their jobs. As the gig economy continues to grow, companies will adjust their structures to this labor trend. For exam-ple, they have to acquire new technology, tools, and processes to ben-efit from the increasing number of gig workers. Many businesses need to adapt their organizational structure to the presence of gig workers. Some businesses may choose a mixed hiring method by recruiting gen-eralists for in-house and using freelancers for some specialist knowledge and skills [42].

The gig work has been beneficial to many gig corporations that take advantage of a global workforce. While many corporations maintain con-trol over the Internet applications they create, they distance themselves from their responsibilities. The result is net profit for these corporations on the back of competitors, nations, governments, municipalities, and communities, and above all, gig workers. On the one hand, they control the apportionment of work, working conditions, prices, work standards, and disciplinary actions. On the other hand, these companies dodge their fair commitments, reject ownership of merchandise bought or sold via their apps, and deny their duties toward workers [47].

At the macroeconomic level, the gig work may increase labor force participation and the number of hours worked in the economy. According to the McKinsey Global Institute studies, the gig economy has increased the labor participation in the United States [11]. The gig work can be beneficial to unemployed, retirees, and students who are seeking some additional sources of income and can ultimately lead them to permanent jobs. Some gig workers can specialize in doing what they do best [26]. Therefore, one may suggest that, by increasing the workers' efficiency, the gig economy may lead to the creation of more productive and satisfying jobs across the globe [11].

References

[1]   Brumm, F. 2016. *Making Gigs Work: The New Economy in Context.* University of Illinois–Urbana Champaign, Master of Human Resources and Industrial Relations.

[2]   Donovan, S.A., D.H. Bradley, and J.O. Shimabukuru. 2016. "What Does the Gig Economy Mean for Workers?" *CONG. RES. SERV. R44365,* available at https://fas.org/sgp/crs/misc/R44365.pdf

[3]   Thomas, K.D. 2018. "Taxing the Gig Economy (June 8, 2017)." *166 University of Pennsylvania Law Review* 1415; *UNC Legal Studies Research Paper.* Available at SSRN: https://ssrn.com/abstract=2894394 or http://dx.doi.org/10.2139/ssrn.2894394

[4]   Cardon, D., and A. Casilli. 2015. "Qu'est-ce que le Digital Labor ?" *Bry-sur-Marne,* INA Éditions.

[5]   Eurofound. 2013. "Self-Employed or Not Self-Employed?" *Working Conditions of 'Economically Dependent Workers.'* Background Paper, Dublin, Eurofound.

[6]   Aloisi, A. 2015. "The Rising of On-Demand Work, A Case Study Research on a Set of Online Platforms and Apps." *Paper Presented at the IV Regulating for Decent Work Conference,* ILO, Geneva, July 8–10, 2015. Available at http://rdw2015.org/download (accessed October 26, 2015).

[7]   De Stefano, V. 2015. "The Rise of the Just-In-Time Workforce: On-Demand Work, Crowdwork, and Labor Protection in the Gig-Economy." *Comp. Lab. L. & Pol'y J.* 37, p. 471.

[8]   James Manyika, June 2015. *A Labour Market that Works: Connecting Talent with Opportunity in the Digital Age.* McKinsey & Company.

[9]   Katz, L.F., and A.B. Krueger. 2016. *The Rise and Nature of Alternative Work Arrangements in the United States,* 1995–2015, (No. w22667). National Bureau of Economic Research.

[10] Intuit. 2015. "Intuit Forecast: 7.6 Million People in On-Demand Economy by 2020." August 13 [Online], available at http://investors.intuit.com/press-releases/press-release-details/2015/Intuit-Forecast-76-Million-People-in-On-Demand-Economy-by-2020/default.aspx

[11] Australian Industry Group. 2016. "The Emergence of the Gig Economy." http://cdn.aigroup.com.au/Reports/2016/Gig_Economy_August_2016.pdf

[12] Kennedy, J.V. 2016. "Three Paths to Update labor law for the Gig Economy." *Information Technology and Innovation Foundation* 18.

[13] Horowitz, S.R. 2015. "Freelancing in America 2015 Report." *Freelancers Union*, October 1, https://freelancersunion.org/blog/dispatches/2015/10/01/freelancing-america-2015/

[14] Harris, S.D., and A.B. Krueger. 2015. "A Proposal for Modernizing Labor Laws for Twenty-First-Century Work: The 'Independent Worker.'" *Discussion Paper 2015-10, The Hamilton Project, The Brookings Institution*, December 2015, http://hamiltonproject.org/assets/files/modernizing_labor_laws_for_twenty_first_century_work_krueger_harris.pdf

[15] Stewart, A., and J. Stanford. 2017. "Regulating Work in the Gig Economy: What are the Options?" *The Economic and Labour Relations Review* 28, no. 3, pp. 420–37.

[16] ESTY. 2016. "Economic Security for the Gig Economy: A Social Safety Net that Works for Everyone Who Works." *Fall* 2016. https://extfiles.etsy.com/advocacy/Etsy_EconomicSecurity_2016.pdf

[17] Federal Reserve Board. 2015. "Report on the Economic Well-Being of U.S. Households in 2014." https://federalreserve.gov/econresdata/2014-report-economic-well-being-us-households-201505.pdf

[18] Katz, L.F., and A.B. Krueger. 2016. "The Rise and Nature of Alternative Work Arrangements in the United States, 1995–2015." http://scholar.harvard.edu/files/lkatz/files/katz_krueger_cws_v3.pdf

[19] Intuit. October 2010. "1Intuit 2020 Report: Twenty Trends that Will Shape the Next Decade."

[20] Gallup. 2013. *Remote Workers Log More Hours and Are Slightly More Engaged.*

[21] Ghayad, R., and W.T. Dickens. 2012. "What Can We Learn by Disaggregating the Unemployment-Vacancy Relationship?"

[22] Krueger, A.B., and J.V. Hall. 2015. *An Analysis of the Labor Market for Uber's Driver-Partners in the United States*, 587. Princeton University Industrial Relations Section Working Paper.

[23] Davis, G.F. 2009. "The Rise and Fall of Finance and the End of the Society of Organizations." *Academy of Management Perspectives* 23, no. 3, pp. 27–44.

[24] Abraham, K.G., and S.K. Taylor. 1996. "Firms' Use of Outside Contractors: Theory and Evidence." *Journal of Labor Economics* 14, no. 3, pp. 394–424.

[25] Cohen, S., and W.B. Eimicke. 2013. *Independent Contracting Policy and Management Analysis*. New York, NY: Columbia University.

[26] Manyika, J., S. Lund, J. Bughin, K. Robinson, J. Mischke, and D. Mahajan. 2016. *Independent Work: Choice, Necessity, and the Gig Economy*. McKinsey & Company.

[27] Etsy. July 2015. *Building an Etsy Economy: The New Face of Creative Entrepreneurship*.

[28] Rudram, B., B. Faith, P. Prieto Martín, and B. Ramalingam. 2016. *Ten Frontier Technologies for International Development*. Brighton: Institute of Development Studies.

[29] Hunt, A., and F. Machingura. 2016. "A Good Gig?" *The Rise of On-Demand Domestic Work*. London, UK: Overseas Development Institute.

[30] Birdsall, N. 2010. "The Middle Class in Developing Countries." In *Equity and Growth in a Globalizing World*, eds. K. Kanbur. and M. Spence. 157–89. Washington: World Bank.

[31] Hindustan Times. 2016. http://hindustantimes.com/more-lifestyle/bai-on-call-how-home-service-apps-changing-the-maids-market/story-s6zz6kmWw1aEamZ1yLxjaL.html, First Published: Feb 21, 2016 14:15 IST

[32] Freedland, M., and N. Kountouris. 2011. *The Legal Construction of Personal Work Relations*. Oxford: Oxford University Press.

[33] Freelancers Union. 2009. "Independent, Innovative, and Unprotected: How the Old Safety Net is Failing America's New Workforce." [Online]. Available: https://fu-res.org/pdfs/advocacy/surveyreport_overview.pdf

[34] Codagnone, C., F. Abadie, and F. Biagi. 2016. "The Future of Work in the 'Sharing Economy.'" *Market Efficiency and Equitable Opportunities or Unfair Precarisation?*

[35] Cherry, M.A., and A. Aloisi. 2016. "Dependent Contractors in the Gig Economy: A Comparative Approach." *Am. UL Rev.* 66, p. 635.

[36] "The New Work Order: Ensuring young Australians have Skills and Experience for the Jobs of the Future, not the Past, Foundation for Young Australians." August 2015.

[37] "The State of Contingent Workforce Management: The 2014–2015 Guidebook." *Ardent*, October 2014.

[38] "The Future, Employees Won't Exist." *Tad Milbourn, Tech Crunch*, June 13, 2015. http://techcrunch.com/2015/06/13/in-the-future-employees-wont-exist/

[39] Online Work Report, Upwork, http://elance-odesk.com/online-work-report-global

[40] "How Hiring International Freelancers Opens The Door To Untapped Talent, Scott Galit, CEO World Magazine." http://ceoworld.biz/2015/07/08/how-hiring-international-freelancers-opens-the-door-to-untapped-talent

[41] "Freelancers are the Future of Hyper-Specialised Teams, Xenios Thrasyvoulou, Wallblog." November 12, 2015. http://wallblog. co.uk/2014/11/12/freelancers-are-the-future-of-hyper-specialised-teams/

[42] "The Rise of the Freelancer: What It Means for Employers and Workers, Sue Barrett, Smart Company." November 2015. http://smartcompany.com. au/marketing/sales/49198-the-rise-of-the-freelancer-what-it-means-for-bosses-and-workers/72http://www.truelancer.com/

[43] Sundararajan, A. 2016. *The Sharing Economy: The End of Employment and the Rise of Crowd-Based Capitalism.* MIT Press.

[44] Friedman, G. 2014. "Workers Without Employers: Shadow Corporations and the Rise of the Gig Economy." *Review of Keynesian Economics* 2, pp. 171–88.

[45] Kenney, M., and J. Zysman. 2016. "The Rise of the Platform Economy." *Issues in Science and Technology* 32, no. 3, pp. 61–69.

[46] Moran, J.A. 2009. "Independent Contractor or Employee-Misclassification of Workers and Its Effect on the State." *Buff. Pub. Int. LJ* 28, p. 105.

[47] Healy, J., D. Nicholson, and A. Pekarek. 2017. "Should We Take the Gig Economy Seriously?" *Labour & Industry: A Journal of the Social and Economic Relations of Work* 27, no. 3, pp. 232–48.

CHAPTER 7

Salient Patterns in the Global Economy

Volatility and Interconnectedness: The Surge in International Trade, FDI, and Structural Imbalances

The Western capitalist economies are, by nature, cyclical and regularly experience the periods of boom and bust, but it seems that, in the recent decades, the capriciousness of capitalism has amplified. The golden age (1950–1970) or the years immediately after the Second World War were marked by constant growth and reconstruction [1]. As we move away from the Second World War, both the frequency and magnitude of recessionary incidents tend to increase. The final years of the 20th century 1995, 1997, 1998, and 1999 are all characterized by major economic or financial crises in Asia, Europe, and North America. The robust economic expansion and trade acceleration in 2000 were followed by an economic contraction in 2001. Finally, in 2008, the United States, Europe,

Asia, and truly most of the world countries experienced the harshest and deepest recession since the 1920s. The mounting volatility in the recent decades is associated with and maybe is caused by another feature, namely, the interconnectedness within the global economy. The economic interconnectedness may be attributed to three major factors: the surge in the international trade, the rise of foreign direct investment across the world particularly in the emerging economies, and serious structural imbalances in the world economy [1].

International Trade has Grown Faster than the World's Output

A salient feature of the global economy in recent decades is the popularity of international trade. Indeed, the growth of international trade has been much faster than the growth of the world output continuously since 1960 [1]. The decline in the cost of transport and telecommunication, and more importantly, the reduction of tariff and non-tariff barriers in the second half of the 20th century resulted in the surge of the international trade of merchandise almost 20-fold [1]. Trade can be considered as both the cause and effect of the global interconnectedness. In other words, the trade flows connect the world countries, and at the same time, the global interconnectedness boosts the international trade. A study conducted by the World Bank reveals that the importance of external trade measured as the ratio of the gross domestic product (GDP) has been constantly growing between the 1960s and 2007 for high-, middle-, and even low-income countries [2]. While it is common to use global trade and international trade interchangeably, it is important to note that international trade is not very much global. Indeed, the trade flows across the world are concentrated in the triade or three regions of Europe, Asia, and North America. Europe is recognized as the world's major trading region, but almost three-quarters of that trade is done across the European countries. It is estimated that 14 percent of the European exports go to North America and Asia. After Europe, Asia is the second most important trade region, but one-half of its trade happens across Asian countries. North America is ranked as the third trade region and conducts almost 50 percent of its trade internally [1].

FDI Has Grown Faster than International Trade

Another feature of the present global economy is the surge of foreign direct investment (FDI) in the past recent decades. The FDI is different from portfolio investment that seeks an only financial return. The FDI is an investment by one firm in another firm with the purpose of gaining some control over that firm's operations. As such, the FDI is an active mode of international business. The growth of FDI has outpaced the growth of both trade and world output. According to the World Bank Investment Report [3], global flows are estimated around 1.8 trillion U.S. dollars in 2017 and are expected to hit 1.85 trillion U.S. dollars in 2018. The spectacular rise in the FDI is an indication of a higher degree of the global interconnectedness, as the world's countries are replacing international trade with an active involvement in foreign business operations. In other words, compared with international trade, the FDI necessitates more cooperation and interconnectedness among the involved corporations and their respective countries. The FDI does not happen directly between two countries; rather, it is conducted via multinational enterprises. Globalization and the subsequent integration of capital markets in the early 1990s contributed to the expansion of FDI. Thus, the surge of FDI is correlated with the trans-nationality of the MNEs. According to the World Bank Investment Report [3], it is possible to identify two main phases of FDI expansion: between 1993 and 1997 and between 2003 and 2010. Despite the differences in national economies, the relative importance of the FDI to domestic economies has increased almost for all countries. This pattern is another indication of higher interconnectedness within the global economy [1].

Structural Imbalances Continue to Swell

The contemporary world economy is marked by significant levels of imbalance that could trigger instability and crises across the planet. Some countries have accumulated significant trade and current account surpluses, while others have added enormous deficits. As a result, those countries with trade surpluses are hoarding huge amounts of capital that they cannot absorb. By contrast, those countries with trade deficits are addicted to higher levels of debt, as they continue to finance their current account by increased borrowing abroad. Ironically, the largest trade deficits are reported in high-income countries, particularly in the United States. The United States alone accounts for more than half the world's current account deficits. The U.S. current account deficit increased from 4.3 percent of GDP in 2000 to an average of 6 percent in 2007 and 2.4 percent in 2017. Because of the global imbalances, those countries with large deficits had to borrow from countries with surpluses and both groups became increasingly dependent on each other. This unhealthy and unstable relationship between borrowers and lenders has been aggravated in recent years and is going to continue in near future.

Geographical Concentration of the Global Economy

In the last few decades, considerable shifts have occurred in the global economic arena, and as a result, the economic standing of several developing countries have improved. For example, the developing economies' shares of the world GDP, exports, and FDI have seen improvement and a group of developing countries, particularly in East Asia, have experienced significant levels of growth. Despite all these transformations, the established developed economies continue to dominate the world economy. We may suggest that the geographies of the global economy in areas such as production, trade, and FDI continue to be highly concentrated. For instance, three-quarters of the global manufacturing and services production, and almost four-fifths of world agricultural production, are concentrated in just 15 countries [1]. Similarly, most of the world's trade and FDI is concentrated in a small number of countries. More than 80 percent of outward FDI originates from 15 countries, while the United States and the United Kingdom accounted for 30 percent of the world total FDI in 2008. Even among the developing economies, there is a high degree of concentration, so only five countries account for more than 50 percent of inward FDI.

The Declining but Still Dominant
Position of the United States

In recent years, the dominance of the United States in the world economy has been declined as the competitors, notably China, and other emerging economies have experienced rapid growth. Most of the decline in the U.S. economy happened between 2003 and 2009 when the economy was hit hard by the deepest recession since the late 1920s [4]. The decline of the U.S. economic influence is reflected particularly in international trade. For instance, the U.S. share of merchandise exports has declined from 17 percent in 1963 to less than 10 percent in the recent years, but its share of merchandise imports has surged from less than 9 percent to 13 percent [1]. In the past decade, the share of U.S. merchandise imports has been growing much faster than its share of merchandise exports, and this has resulted in a growing trade deficit. The trade imbalance between the United States and China is so significant that China is acting like America's lender through its huge holdings of the U.S. Treasury bonds. Furthermore, the position of the U.S. economy has been declining with regard to the FDI. The share of the U.S. in the world's FDI has declined from 50 percent in the 1960s to less than 20 percent currently [1]. Another interesting observation is that inward investment is becoming increasingly important to the U.S. economy. The inward FDI used to be only a tiny fraction of the country's outward FDI, but now the U.S. economy has become a more important destination of FDI. This inverse relationship between the inward and outward FDI flows could be attributed to the country's trade imbalances.

Despite the rise of emerging economies in the past two decades, the United States remains the unquestionable dominant nation in the global economy. Relying on its main technological, military, geographical, and human resources, the United States will be able to keep its dominance at least for the next two decades. With less than 5 percent of the world's population, the United States accounts for almost 23 percent of the world GDP at market exchange rates and over 19 percent at purchasing power parity (PPP) exchange rates [5]. The U.S. economy is larger than the next four largest economies altogether, namely, China, Japan, Germany, and the United Kingdom. Based on the standard of living, we find similar results. While standards of living are rising and poverty is declining for millions of people in emerging countries, the United States continues to be ahead by a long way. The standard of living in the United States is on average four times higher than that in Brazil, six times higher than that in China, and as much as 15 times higher than that in India. Currently, the U,S, economy accounts for 30 percent of the world's GDP, 20 percent of the world manufacturing production, 28 percent of the global service production, and 8 percent of the global agricultural production. The United States is still the world's biggest foreign direct investor, the largest exporter of commercial services and agricultural products, and the third largest exporter of manufactured goods [1]. Perhaps, one of the most important advantages of the United States over all other nations resides in its control over the global financial system, particularly by imposing dollar as the reserve currency. Through a dollar-based international monetary system, the United States is practically taxing every other state, so, it is able to reap more than it pays out in the provision of public goods [6]. The emerging economies like China, India, and Brazil are large, but are not necessarily efficient and competitive in comparison with the United States. According to the World Economic Forum surveys, the United States has been one of the most competitive economies of the world for the past decade, while China, Russia, India, and Brazil have occupied the ranks on the bottom of the list [7]. Closely associated with competitiveness is the capacity of an economy to innovate. Innovation is perhaps the most outstanding strength of America. The United States accounted for 40 percent of the total world research and development in 2008. The United States remains the most innovative country in the world, with more patents than all other countries combined. Finally, the United States is benefiting from strong and highly competitive corporations. In 2011, 25 of the top 50 corporations were American [8]. By contrast, the emerging countries' multinationals remain mainly dependent on natural resources and government support.

Europe: Dominance, Diversity, and Gradual Decline

Europe has been evolving in the past five centuries through industrialization and colonization and has deeply influenced human civilization. Many modern international institutions and organizations are originated in Western Europe, particularly in countries like Britain, France, and Germany. Therefore, the European countries in conjunction with the United States are benefiting from a great advantage in designing, affecting, and enforcing the international rules in the areas of security, cooperation, finance, trade, culture, sport, science, and technology. With 28 member states (27 excluding Britain), 510 million inhabitants, a GDP of 19.7 trillion U.S. dollars [9], and a rich cultural heritage, the European Union (EU) is certainly an important power on the world stage. In terms of GDP, the EU is the biggest economic power in the world. Europe is the world's biggest trading area and the primary destination and origin of the global FDI. The European continent and even the EU represent economically diverse countries that have experienced uneven rates of economic growth in the past two decades. Even the effects of the financial crisis of 2007–2008 were very different across Europe. While some peripheral countries such as Portugal, Spain, Italy, and Greece experienced harsh downturns, other Western European nations, particularly Germany, were not affected very much. Germany is and will remain the biggest and the most competitive economy in Europe. After the United States, China, and Japan, Germany boasts its position as the fourth largest manufacturing economy. It is the largest manufacturing exporter and the third largest commercial service exporter in the world. Furthermore, Germany is the third most important source of the FDI [1]. The European countries show dissimilar patterns in external trade. For instance, Germany, the Netherlands and Sweden generally generate merchandise trade surpluses, while France, the United Kingdom, Spain, and Italy have merchandise trade deficits. On the other hand, the United Kingdom has a big service trade surplus; France and Spain have modest service trade surpluses, while Germany has a considerable service trade deficit. A very serious challenge in Europe is about the viability of the single currency and the underlying fiscal and monetary policies at the national level [10]. The single currency crises made the EU economic model less attractive not only to the member states, but also to a large number of the EU citizens. Regardless of the economic and institutional differences across the European countries, Europe is an attractive destination for FDI inflows and a resourceful home for outward FDI flows [1].

Transitional Economies: Eastern Europe and Russia

After the fall of the Berlin Wall and the collapse of the Soviet Union in the early 1990s, the Eastern European countries and Russia took drastic measures to move from centrally planned economic systems to market-based economic models. This group of transitional economies faced major institutional, cultural, and economic hurdles in their move toward market-based capitalistic economies. Their heavy manufacturing industries were not competitive at the global level, they lacked adequate institutional structures, and more importantly, they were not culturally prepared for such a sweeping transition. Consequently, many of these transitional economies faltered and experienced significant contractions in their GDP. For instance, the share of the Soviet Union of the world manufacturing production fell from 10 percent in 1985 to only 1 percent in the mid-1990s [11]. The so-called group of transitional economies is heterogonous and represents significant differences with regard to economic development, growth, and competitiveness. The four important economies of this group are the Russian Federation, Poland, the Czech Republic, and Hungary, whose combined share of global GDP is almost 4 percent and accounts for most of the manufacturing production and exports [1]. In the past decade, Poland, the Czech Republic, and Hungary have joined the EU and have shown promising signs of growth. Russia is on a different path, as it has been relying heavily on the natural resources to fuel its economy, and more recently, has been at odds with the West over its geopolitical interests in Ukraine, Syria, and the Middle East. Since 2013, many Russian businesses and officials have been facing the Western sanctions due to the Russian meddling in Ukraine and the annexation of Crimea.

Continuous Ascendance in the Asia Pacific: The China Effect

The most important shift in the global economy in the past three decades is the rise of Asian countries, particularly China, Japan, Korea, and India. The rise of Asia started in Japan after the Second World War. The pace of growth in Japan was so remarkable that the Japanese economy climbed from the fifth rank in the early 1960s to the second rank in the 1980s. Similarly, Japan's share of the global FDI jumped from 1 percent in the 1960s to 12 percent in the 1990s. This spectacular growth in Japan paved the way for other Asian countries. Hong Kong, Korea, Singapore, and

Taiwan dubbed as *the four tigers* emerged as newly industrialized countries. The wave of economic growth continued later by the rise of the second tier of East Asian developing economies, namely, Indonesia, Malaysia, and Thailand. In the early 1980s, after the major economic reforms in China and India, these two countries embarked on a wave of fast economic growth that continued for more than three decades. Despite all the devastating effects of the financial crisis of 1997–1998, most of the East Asian economies proved to be resilient, as they resumed their above-average growth soon after.

Between 1980 and 2007, China pursued an active export strategy to fuel an astonishing economic growth, averaging 10 percent a year. China has stimulated its economy by relying on a competitive manufacturing industry, which has benefited from the cheap and abundant workforce. This model of economic growth could be less practical in the long term, as the country is already witnessing higher wages, shrinking workforce, and improving working conditions that ultimately will reduce its manufacturing competitiveness. Furthermore, the Chinese manufacturing model is dependent on the consumption of huge amounts of fossil fuel and lax environmental standards that will not be sustainable in the long run [12]. Substantial socioeconomic changes are essential in order for China's growth to be sustainable. Indeed, transitioning from middle- to high-income levels is generally more challenging than moving up from low- to middle-income levels. The sustainability of growth is a top priority in China, and for that reason, China has started to modernize its economy by allocating more funding to research and development. The modernization of the education system and labor force implies that China may boost its economic growth by relying on knowledge-based sectors instead of cheap labor manufacturing. Chinese economic growth is likely to be affected significantly by the demographic trends. As a result of China's one-child policy that was introduced in 1977, a large portion of the population will grow old together, putting a huge pressure on many segments, including the labor market, pension plans, education, and healthcare services. As China is moving away from cheap labor manufacturing, the negative effects of population shrinking may be mitigated by automation, innovation, and shift to a knowledge-based economy [13]. The transition of China from a poor, undeveloped, and agrarian society to a world power may pose serious threats to the old Western hegemony in the international system. On the one hand, China is overtly challenging the American influence in the Asia Pacific region [14]. On the other hand, China has been encouraging regional cooperation processes that do not include the United States. For example, the Shanghai Cooperation Organization made up of China, Russia, Uzbekistan, Kyrgyzstan, Kazakhstan, and Tajikistan has become a platform for Chinese influence [15]. The Shanghai Cooperation Organization's goals in international affairs are principally the same goals found in the foreign policy directives of China [16]. Likewise, China is raising its involvement in ASEAN to gain regional influence [17]. In the past few years, China has been developing strategies toward resource- and energy-rich countries in Africa, Asia, and Latin America [20]. By challenging the American and Western hegemony, China has been developing some privileged economic and political relations with countries like Burma, Sudan, Zimbabwe, and Iran. Similarly, China has become Africa's single largest trading partner, as Chinese businesses have established a significant presence in Africa by building infrastructure and running mines and oil fields [18]. After the financial crisis of 2008, Chinese multinationals have embarked on mergers and acquisitions in Europe and Latin America to promote their global expansion [19]. More recently, Chinese multinationals are becoming world leaders in major industries such as banking, engineering, and construction, mining and oil production, metals and telecommunications.

India: The Steady Growth

The economic importance of India resides in its large and rapidly growing population, which is estimated at 1.3 billion and is poised to surpass China in the next five years. After implementing the economic reform in the 1980s, India has experienced a consistent period of high economic growth, averaging at 5 percent per year [21]. While the economic growth in India has been constantly above the world average at between 5 and 6 percent, it has been almost half that of China during the last two decades [1]. The interesting point is that the gap between the Chinese and India economic growth rates have been shrinking in recent years, indicating that the growth in India may be finally gaining steam. According to the World

Bank and IMF, the significant economic growth of India is expected to continue in the next few years [12]. India is already a member of the G20. While the Indian economy is the same size as those of Brazil and Russia, what makes India different is its huge potential for a sustainable growth until 2020 at an annual average rate of 8 percent [12]. If the Indian economy grows as expected, then it will be larger than the U.S. economy in 2050 [12]. In order to maintain future economic growth, India needs to continue reforms and improve multiple areas, including education, agriculture, and infrastructure [22]. India's weakness is seen particularly in manufacturing. Despite its vast human resources, India is ranked as the world's 14th largest manufacturing economy, and the country is not even on the list of top 15 merchandise exporters. India's manufacturing is not competitive at all. The main engine of the Indian economy is the service sector, and particularly information technology that accounts for 35 percent of India's exports whose revenue has increased from 3.3 billion in 1998 to an enormous 87 billion in 2008. Despite this phenomenal growth, India is still a very poor country that grapples with various economic and social problems. According to the United Nations reports, almost 33 percent of India's population lives below the one-dollar-a-day (PPP) poverty line, and almost 70 percent live on less than two dollars per day [23]. By 2050, India is expected to have a per capita income that is still only 55 percent that of China, despite the fact that the Indian GDP per capita growth rates are expected to exceed Chinese rates by 2020–2025 [24]. A poor infrastructure, high illiteracy levels, weak currency, high inflation rates, low agricultural productivity, and small manufacturing sector are the main hurdles that constrain Indian economic growth [23]. Overall, India has the potential to become a major economic power comparable to China, but at present, it remains an emerging economy that is underperforming China and Asian tigers.

Latin America: Lagging Behind

In the past two decades, the Latin American and Caribbean countries have been lagging behind the emerging economies in Asia and Eastern Europe [25]. Latin American countries are generally rich in natural resources, and some like Brazil, Mexico, and Argentina have benefitted from a long history of industrialization. For instance, Brazil is the fifth largest country in the world with a population of more than 200 million, and a GDP of 3.2 trillion U.S. dollars, ranked as the 8th largest economy in the world in 2017 (World Bank). Similarly, Mexico, with a population of 127 million and a GDP of 2.4 trillion U.S. dollars, was ranked as the 15th largest economy in the world in 2017 (World Bank). Despite all these resources, most of the Latin American economies have underperformed in the past two decades due to multiple factors, including sizeable informal sectors, poor infrastructures, corruption, lack of education attainment, and restricted competition. None of the Latin American countries has shown a significant export performance, so we can claim that, in the past 20 years, the Latin American region has been lagging behind the East Asian economies in the export of merchandise. Mexico has highly benefited from the North American Free Trade agreement and its access to the Canadian and American markets. Apart from some significant export growth in the 1990s, the Mexican economy has constantly underperformed. Mexico's GDP growth rate between 2000 and 2007 has been the lowest among the Latin American major economies [1]. Despite the NAFTA membership and its proximity to the United States, Mexico has been outcompeted by Chinese manufacturing. This trend is likely to continue in near future, as the Chinese exporters are constantly climbing the ladder of technological and operational sophistication. Similarly, Brazil is underperforming all other BRICS countries, including China, Russia, India, and South Africa. Despite a long history of industrialization, Brazil's role in the global economy is mainly restricted to natural resources and commodities, including agriculture and mining products. Brazil is resource rich and is dependent on the export of commodities such as sugar, soybeans, orange juice, coffee, tobacco, beef, cotton, chicken, and pork. The country is an agricultural powerhouse and has the largest agricultural trade surplus in the world [26]. This high level of dependence on commodities makes the Brazilian economy vulnerable to fluctuations in commodity prices.

References

[1] Dicken, P. 2007. *Global Shift: Mapping the Changing Contours of the World Economy.* Sage Publications Ltd.

[2]   Kaplinsky, R. 2001. "Is Globalization All It Is Cracked Up to be?" *Review of International Political Economy* 8, no. 1, pp. 45–65.

[3]   United Nations Conference on Trade and Development. 2017. *World Investment Report 2017: Investment and the Digital Economy.* UN.

[4]   Clark, G. L., & Wójcik, D. (Eds.). (2018). *The New Oxford Handbook of Economic Geography.* Oxford University Press.

[5]   Wade, R.H. 2011. "Emerging World Order? From Multipolarity to Multilateralism in the G20, the World Bank, and the IMF." *Politics & Society* 39, no. 3, pp. 347–78.

[6]   Norrlof, C. 2010. *America's Global Advantage: US Hegemony and International Cooperation.* Cambridge University Press.

[7]   Galama, T., and J. Hosek. 2008. *US Competitiveness in Science and Technology.* Rand Corporation.

[8]   Cox, M. 2012. "Power Shifts, Economic Change and the Decline of the West?" *International Relations* 26, no. 4, pp. 369–88.

[9]   First Population Estimates, 2016. Eurostat—Population on January 1, 2016. Retrieved July 11, 2016.

[10]   Smith, K.E. 2013. "Can the European Union be a Pole in a Multipolar World?" *The International Spectator* 48, no. 2, pp. 114–26.

[11]   Cox, M. 2012. "Power Shifts, Economic Change and the Decline of the West?" *International Relations* 26, no. 4, pp. 369–88.

[12]   Stefánsson, O.I.N. 2012. *The BRICs and International Relations: An Assessment of the Potential Leaders in a Global Future.*

[13]   Sachs, G. 2007. *BRICS and Beyond.* Goldman Sachs Global Economics Group.

[14]   Desker, B. 2008. "New Security Dimensions in the Asia–Pacific." *Asia Pacific Review* 15, no. 1, pp. 56–75.

[15]   Gu, J., J. Humphrey, and D. Messner. 2008. "Global Governance and Developing Countries: The Implications of the Rise of China." *World Development* 36, no. 2, pp. 274–92.

[16]   Harden, B.E. 2014. "The Diplomatic Ambitions of the BRIC State: Challenging the Hegemony of the West." *Journal of International Relations and Foreign Policy* 2, no. 2, pp. 1–18.

[17]   "Asia's never-Closer Union." 2010. *The Economist*, February 4, http://economist.com/world/asia/displaystory.cfm?story_id=15452622 (accessed March 10, 2010).

[18]   Taylor, I. 2008. "China in Africa by Alden Chris London: Zed Books, 2007. Pp. 136, £ 12.99 (pbk)." *The Journal of Modern African Studies* 46, no. 2, pp. 325–26.

[19]   OECD. 2017. "Business Insights on Emerging Markets 2017." *OECD Development Centre*, Paris. http://oecd.org/dev/oecdemnet.htm

[20] Yeung, H.W. 2004. *Chinese Capitalism in a Global Era: Towards Hybrid Capitalism*. London: Routledge.

[21] Poddar, T., and E. Yi. 2007. "India's Rising Growth Potential." In *BRICs and Beyond*, ed. G. Sachs, 11. New York, NY: Global Economics Group.

[22] O'Neill, J., and T. Poddar. June 16, 2008. "Ten Things for India to Achieve its 2050 Potential." *Goldman Sachs Global Economic Paper* 169, nos. 3–5. www2.goldmansachs.com/ideas/brics/howsolid-doc.pdf (accessed February 23, 2010).

[23] Degaut, M., and C.E. Meacham. 2015. "Do the BRICS Still Matter?" *Center for Strategic & International Studies*.

[24] Murphy, C.N., and J. Yates. 2009. *The International Organization for Standardization (ISO) Global Governance through Voluntary Consensus*. Routledge.

[25] Phillips, N. 2009. "Migration as Development Strategy? The New Political Economy of Dispossession and Inequality in the Americas." *Review of International Political Economy* 16, no. 2, pp. 231–59.

[26] Beattie, A. 2005. "Top of the Crops: Brazil's Huge Heartland is Yielding Farms that can Feed the World." *Financial Times* 23, no. 6, p. 2005.

CHAPTER 8

Consumers and Consumption

1. Surge in the Global Middle Class and the Shift of Consumption from West to East
2. The Growing Importance of Cities as Centers of Consumption
3. The Shortening Product Lifecycles
4. Digitization of Consumption
5. Consumers' Attention as a Precious Commodity

Surge in the Global Middle Class and the Shift of Consumption from West to East

Behind the economic performance of the developed countries and their significant consumers' markets are sizeable middle classes. The middle-class citizens usually enjoy a decent level of financial security, and as a result, conduct a comfortable life marked by access to stable housing, decent healthcare and educational opportunities, reasonable retirement, and discretionary income that can be spent on vacation and leisure pursuits [1]. The middle class is an ambiguous social classification and may involve different meanings across the world, but we may simply suggest that the middle-class citizens are those who can have a relatively comfortable life. The importance of middle class resides particularly in its consumerism and in its constant desire for acquiring high-quality and differentiated products. The middle-class consumers often are willing to pay for quality and differentiation [2]. In the 20th century and the early decades of the 21st century, the middle-class consumers of North America and Europe have been responsible for generating demand, while low- and middle-income citizens in Asia have been the main source of supply.

Currently, 1.8 billion people or 28 percent of the world's population are categorized as middle-class citizens. Half of the middle-class people live in developed economies. The middle-class citizens are concentrated in North America (338 million), Europe (664 million), and Asia (525 million) [1]. The United States, the European Union, and Japan with, respectively, 230, 450, and 125 million middle-class consumers are at the top of the list. By contrast, there are very few middle-class consumers, approximately 32 million in sub-Saharan Africa. Obviously, the middle class is a broad category, and there are significant differences between the purchasing power of middle-class consumers in the United States, Europe, Africa, and China. For instance, the United States is home to 12 percent of the world's middle-class people, but it accounts for 21 percent or 4.4 trillion U.S. dollars of the global spending by middle-class consumers [1].

Currently, the vast majority of the world's population or almost 70 percent are categorized as poor. Over the next 20 years, this pattern is expected to change, as the world's population will become richer and the share of the middle class will increase substantially. For instance, by 2022, more people in the world will be middle class than the poor, and by 2030, five billion people or two-thirds of the global population could be categorized as middle class. According to the World Bank's Global Economic Prospects, the global middle class would expand from 7.6 percent of the world's population in 2000 to between 16.1 and 19.4 percent of the world's population by 2030 [3]. Goldman Sachs estimated that the global middle class is expected to increase from 29 percent of the world population in 2008 to 50 percent in 2030 [4]. In the same way, the global spending of the middle class could increase from 21 trillion U.S. dollars in 2009 to 56 trillion U.S. dollars by 2030.

Due to the accelerated economic growth in Asia, and particularly in China, the center of gravity of global output is expected to shift from the West to Asia involving that the Asian countries, notably China, India, Indonesia, and Vietnam, will account for a larger share of the world economy [5]. Therefore, there will be a major shift in the distribution of wealth from the western developed countries to Asia (see Figures 8.1 and 8.2). Some studies suggest that almost all of the new members of the global middle class will live in Asia [1]. In the next 20 years, the

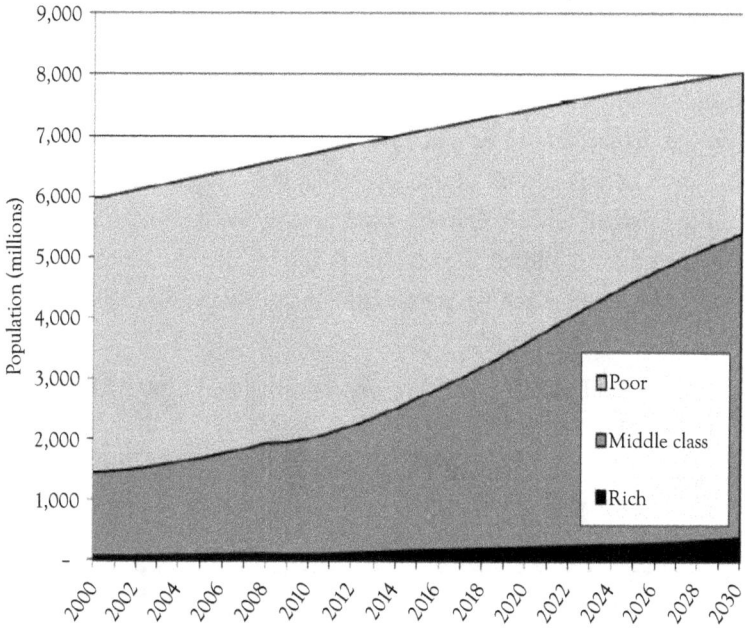

Figure 8.1 A surge in the global middle class

Source: [1].

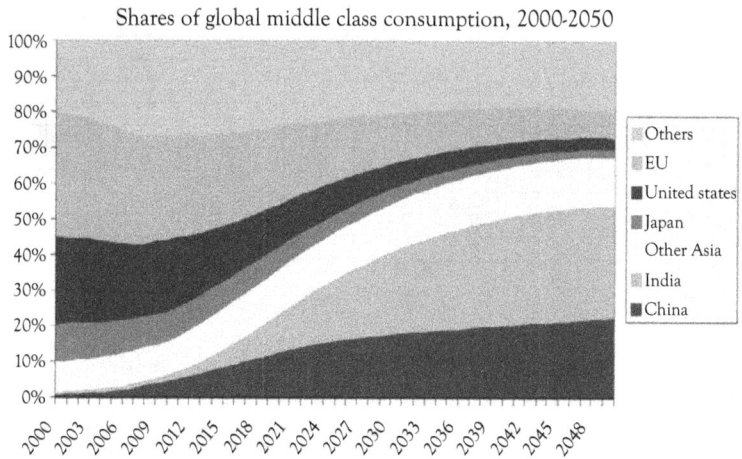

Figure 8.2 India and China make waves in the global middle class

Source: [5].

number of middle-class consumers may increase six-fold from the current 500 million to more than 3.2 billion. The share of Asian middle-class consumers will increase from one-quarter to two-thirds by 2030. By contrast, the share of North America and Europe can drop from 54 percent to 17 percent for the same period (see Tables 8.1, 8.2, and 8.3).

The Asian middle-class growth is remarkably rapid. By 2030, Asia will be home to three billion middle-class people, which are 10 times more than North America and five times more than Europe. Asia's share of the

Table 8.1 Total middle-class consumption, regions, (2005 PPP$, billions and global share)

	2009		2020		2030	
North America	5,602	26%	5,863	17%	5,837	10%
Europe	8,138	38%	10,301	29%	11,337	20%
Central and South America	1,534	7%	2,315	7%	3,117	6%
Asia Pacific	4,952	23%	14,798	42%	32,596	59%
Sub-Saharan Africa	256	1%	448	1%	827	1%
Middle East and North Africa	796	4%	1,321	4%	1,966	4%
World	21,278	100%	35,045	100%	55,680	100%

Source: [1].

Table 8.2 Total middle-class consumption, top 10 countries (2005 PPP$, billions and global share)

	2009			2020			2030		
1	United States	4,377	21%	China	4,468	13%	India	12,777	23%
2	Japan	1,800	8%	United States	4,270	12%	China	9,985	18%
3	Germany	1,219	6%	India	3,733	11%	United States	3,969	7%
4	France	927	4%	Japan	2,203	6%	Indonesia	2,474	4%
5	United Kingdom	889	4%	Germany	1,361	4%	Japan	2,286	4%
6	Russia	870	4%	Russia	1,189	3%	Russia	1,448	3%
7	China	859	4%	France	1,077	3%	Germany	1,335	2%
8	Italy	740	3%	Indonesia	1,020	3%	Mexico	1,239	2%
9	Mexico	715	3%	Mexico	992	3%	Brazil	1,225	2%
10	Brazil	623	3%	United Kingdom	976	3%	France	1,119	2%

Source: [1].

Table 8.3 Spending by the global middle class, 2009 to 2030 (millions of 2005 PPP dollars)

	2009		2020		2030	
North America	5602	26%	5863	17%	5837	10%
Europe	8138	38%	10301	29%	11337	20%
Central and South America	1534	7%	2315	7%	3117	6%
Asia Pacific	4952	23%	14798	42%	32596	59%
Sub-Saharan Africa	256	1%	448	1%	827	1%
Middle East and North Africa	796	4%	1321	4%	1966	4%
World	21278	100%	35045	100%	55680	100%

Source: [1].

global middle class' spending may increase from 23 percent in 2009 to 59 percent by 2030 [1]. By 2020 and 2030, China and India could be ranked among the top three countries with regard to the middle-class spending surpassing the United States [1]. Thus, the global consumer market is changing fast. For example, as of 2000, the United States accounted for 37 percent of global car sales, while China accounted for barely 1 percent. By 2020, China is expected to account for 25 percent of the global car market [6]. This phenomenon is not limited to China, as other developing economies are on the same path. In the next decade, the share of developing economies in the global middle class will surpass the share of advanced countries. For instance, the middle class in Latin America is expected to grow from 181 million to 313 million by 2030. In Africa and the Middle East, the middle class is expected to more than double, from 137 million to 341 million [7]. In the past decade, private consumption in developing economies has been growing at about three times the rate of advanced countries, and this surge in consumption is expected to increase even further [8]. Developing economies are showing the rapid growth of demand for all discretionary products from cars, electronics, and cell phones to toothpaste and air conditioners. Consequently, there will be a tectonic consumption shift from the West to the East, and the products, fashions, tastes, and designs are expected to be adapted to the new global middle class' preferences. A large number of middle-class consumers in the East will shape global consumption.

The Growing Importance of Cities as Centers of Consumption

Over the course of the past three decades, the world has experienced a wave of fast urbanization. The world's population is becoming more urbanized than ever, and big cities are attracting a large number of inhabitants. For the first time in 2007, the world's urban population surpassed the world's rural population. According to the World Bank reports, the share of the world's urban population has risen from 30 percent in 1950 to more than 54 percent in 2015. The ongoing urbanization in conjunction with the growth of the global population will add 2.5 billion people to the urban population by 2050, with nearly 90 percent of the increase concentrated in Asia and Africa [9]. In the age of globalization, the economic activity is becoming highly clustered around urban centers. Almost all manufacturing, logistics, distribution, employment, healthcare, financial and business services, and by extension, demand and spending are located in urban places. A few cities are becoming responsible for much of the national economic activity. Within every country, we find out significant disparities between urban and regional economies, in terms of their specialization, growth rates, and future prospects. In some countries, one or two major cities dominate the national economies. In some others, a few large and mid-sized cities determine the dynamism of the national economies. Some cities are so integrated into the global economy that transcends their respective national borders and acts as quasi-independent economic players [10]. By 2030, the world is expected to have 41 megacities with more than 10 million inhabitants [11]. Currently, 29 megacities are home to 471 million people, an equivalent of 6 percent of the world's total population [12] (see Table 8.4). Furthermore, the number of cities with populations over 20 million is increasing fast. As shown in Figure 8.3, a relatively small number of cities are dominating the global economic arena because of their active involvement in business occupations such as financial and business services, and corporate control and coordination functions (see Figure 8.4) [13]. In the developed economies of the West, urbanization is a well-established phenomenon that experienced much of its growth in the 1950s and 1960s [14]. By contrast, urbanization in developing economies is a new phenomenon that accelerated only after the 1990s. Currently, more than 75 percent of the populations in developing economies still live in rural areas, suggesting that the sharpest increase in the urban centers will happen in such countries [15]. Based on the United Nations estimates, almost 2.5 billion people will be added to the global urban population between 2014 and 2050. Of these 2.5 billion new urban dwellers, almost 90 percent will live in Africa and Asia. Only three countries, namely India, China, and Nigeria, are expected to account for more than one-third of the global urban population growth [16].

The recent population movement from rural areas to cities in China, India, and other developing or emerging economies creates huge opportunities for marketers. By 2030, consumers in large cities will account for half of the global population and will generate 81 percent of the global

Table 8.4 Top cities by absolute consumption and consumption growth

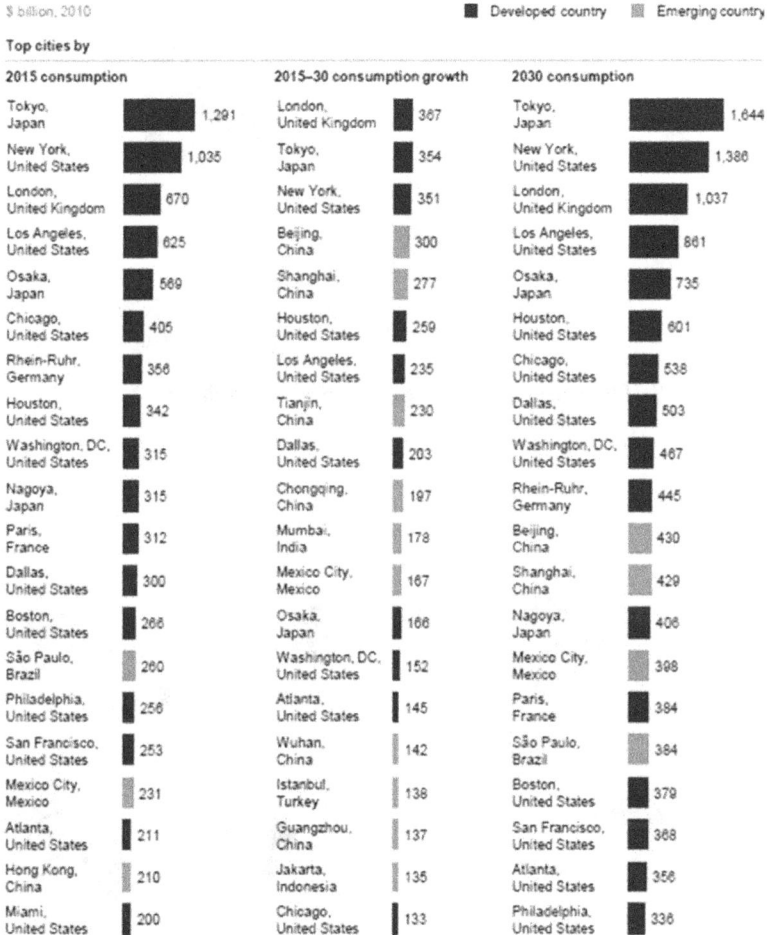

$ billion, 2010   ■ Developed country   ▨ Emerging country

Top cities by

2015 consumption		2015–30 consumption growth		2030 consumption	
Tokyo, Japan	1,291	London, United Kingdom	367	Tokyo, Japan	1,644
New York, United States	1,035	Tokyo, Japan	354	New York, United States	1,386
London, United Kingdom	670	New York, United States	351	London, United Kingdom	1,037
Los Angeles, United States	625	Beijing, China	300	Los Angeles, United States	861
Osaka, Japan	569	Shanghai, China	277	Osaka, Japan	735
Chicago, United States	405	Houston, United States	259	Houston, United States	601
Rhein-Ruhr, Germany	356	Los Angeles, United States	235	Chicago, United States	538
Houston, United States	342	Tianjin, China	230	Dallas, United States	503
Washington, DC, United States	315	Dallas, United States	203	Washington, DC, United States	467
Nagoya, Japan	315	Chongqing, China	197	Rhein-Ruhr, Germany	445
Paris, France	312	Mumbai, India	178	Beijing, China	430
Dallas, United States	300	Mexico City, Mexico	167	Shanghai, China	429
Boston, United States	266	Osaka, Japan	166	Nagoya, Japan	406
São Paulo, Brazil	260	Washington, DC, United States	152	Mexico City, Mexico	398
Philadelphia, United States	256	Atlanta, United States	145	Paris, France	384
San Francisco, United States	253	Wuhan, China	142	São Paulo, Brazil	384
Mexico City, Mexico	231	Istanbul, Turkey	138	Boston, United States	379
Atlanta, United States	211	Guangzhou, China	137	San Francisco, United States	368
Hong Kong, China	210	Jakarta, Indonesia	135	Atlanta, United States	356
Miami, United States	200	Chicago, United States	133	Philadelphia, United States	336

Source: [17].

consumption [17]. From a marketing perspective, we may suggest that the urban world is where consumption takes place. Consumers in large cities will account for 81 percent of the global consumption by 2030 and 91 percent of consumption growth between 2015 and 2030. What is more interesting is that global urban consumption is highly concentrated. Only 100 cities will account for 45 percent of consumption growth, and 32 of them will account for a quarter of the global total (23 trillion U.S. dollars) between 2015 and 2030 [18]. The growth in urban consumption

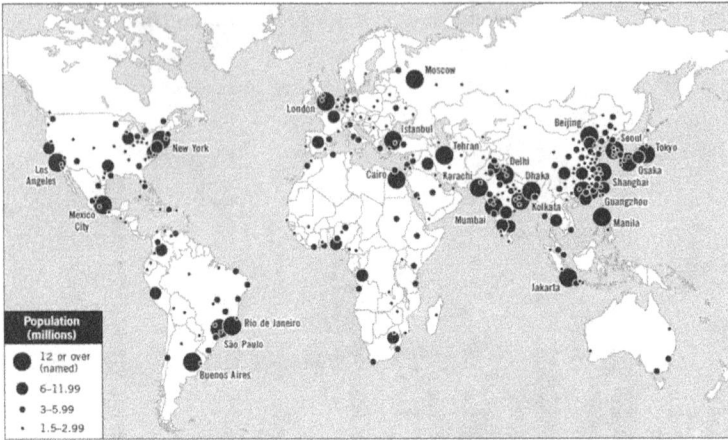

Figure 8.3 The world's major cities by size of population

Source: citypopulation.de

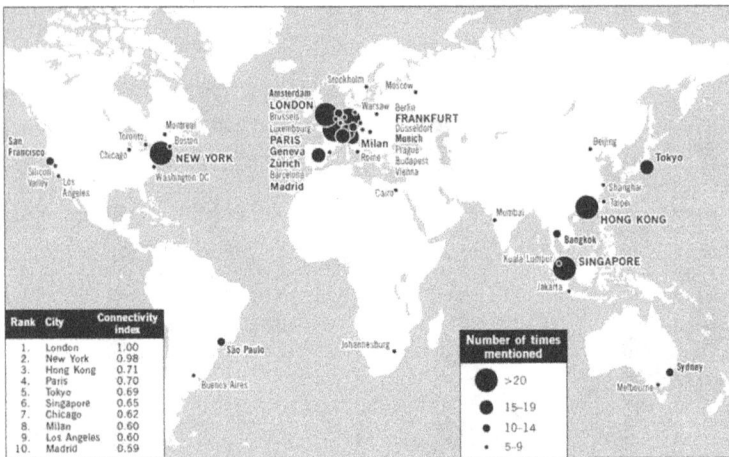

Figure 8.4 Key cities in the global economy

Source: [13].

is related to the consumption of services and amenities in cities, including growing expenditures for entertainment, restaurants, and travel. Many multinational corporations are developing strategies to serve the world's new urban consumers more effectively. According to the Deloitte's Globalization Survey (2013), around 50 percent of the companies have already developed customized strategies for specific cities [19]. Underlying their business strategies is the financial power of urban centers and the affluence of their residents. Large cities in emerging countries are rapidly claiming their place alongside the long-established cities of the developed world. From a marketing standpoint, the urban centers in emerging or developing economies are more attractive as they are growing faster than their counterparts in developed economies are (see Figures 8.3 and 8.4).

Table 8.4 lists the cities with the highest consumption and the consumption growth between 2015 and 2030. As shown in the figure, the top five cities with the largest projected growth in consumption are London (367 billion U.S. dollars), Tokyo (354 billion U.S. dollars), New York (351 billion U.S. dollars), Beijing (300 billion U.S. dollars), and Shanghai (277 billion U.S. dollars). As shown in Figure 8.4, of the 20 cities with the largest predicted increase in consumption between 2015 and 2030, seven are located in the United States, six are in China, and two are in Japan. The following cities will have the largest consumption by 2030: Tokyo (Japan), New York (United States), London (United Kingdom), Los Angeles (United States), Osaka (Japan), Houston (United States), Chicago (United States), Dallas (United States), Washington, DC (United States), Rhein-Ruhr (Germany), Beijing (China), Shanghai (China), Nagoya (Japan), Mexico City (Mexico), Paris (France), São Paulo (Brazil), Boston (United States), San Francisco (United States), Atlanta (United States), and Philadelphia (United States).

The Shortening Product Lifecycles

The product lifecycle is a useful concept that describes the sales history of the product over its lifetime. Generally, the product lifecycle is presented as a bell-shaped curve and is divided into some major stages, including introduction, growth, maturity, and decline. During the last stage or decline stage, the more innovative and competitive products replace the old ones. In recent decades, businesses have come under growing pressure from investors and consumers to innovate and introduce their products faster. As a result, the pace of innovation has substantially accelerated, and product lifecycles have continued to shorten. We are witnessing a growing temporal acceleration in production, purchase, and consumption processes. On the one hand, the temporal acceleration pushes manufacturers to create more innovative and performing products because there is only a narrow opportunity to earn profits before the competition catches up. On the other hand, the temporal acceleration pushes the consumers to rush and buy the latest products to fulfill their lives by consuming faster than ever. The temporal acceleration destroys stability by making the items such as electronic devices obsolete shortly after their introduction. The average lifespan of a computer has shrunk from four or five years to two years in the past decade. That is why a large proportion of sales in electronic devices happen soon after the introduction of the product. As trade becomes more global, new products and technologies have the potential to reach a larger number of users in shorter periods. For example, while it took the telephone almost 70 years to reach 80 percent penetration in the U.S. households, it would take only 12 to 15 years for smartphones to reach the same level of penetration [20]. The shortening product lifecycle pushes companies to keep low inventory levels and minimize investments at every point in their value chain [21]. The speedy manufacturing is expected at all stages of production, including supply chains and technological development. As the product lifecycles shorten, the introduction and growth stages of the product lifecycle are merged and are followed immediately by a steep decline. In other words, the shortening product lifecycles indicate the lack of a maturity stage. In other words, a narrow space of opportunity exists to make profits on a new product before the competition catches up and margins decline. The sharp decline in the product lifecycle and sudden shift of users to the next generation products means that businesses may lack time and resources to reach out to all their potential users. Hence, businesses are often caught in a situation where a new product replaces the old ones before they are able to conduct their marketing campaign [22]. To deal with the effects of the shortening product lifecycle, firms can consider three marketing strategies: extensive marketing effort, simultaneous appeal to various segments, and intensive marketing effort. Shortening product lifecycle means that firms have a small amount of time to conduct their marketing campaigns and reach potential customers [23]. When selling products with shorter lifecycles, businesses should collect and process information for various segments quickly and simultaneously. Finally, firms should conduct more intensive and high-quality marketing campaigns to increase the number of customers [23].

Digitization of Consumption

In the past decade, we have been witnessing a significant intersection between consumption and advanced information technologies. Because of technological advances, physical and virtual environments are rapidly converging, and companies are required to satisfy customers' needs and desires more quickly. Customers are benefiting from an infinite number of online and off-line options for researching and buying new products and services at their fingertips, and digital devices have become indispensable for executing promotions, stimulating sales, and increasing market share [24]. Thanks to new information technologies, the consumers are gaining control of their interactions with businesses [25]. At the same time, customers are demanding instantaneous and continuous digital experience from businesses. We witness that both business-to-consumer and business-to-business customers are developing their expectations of product or service quality around the speed, convenience, and ease of use [26]. Customers are raising their expectations by referring to companies such as Amazon and Apple. They expect that any other business delivers products and services with rapidity, convenience, and ease of use compared to the tech giants. In dealing with the increasing pressure of consumption digitization, businesses focus on three main areas to attract and retain their customers: customer experience, personalization, and ownership to access [26]. First, customer experience is becoming an important variable in addition to the quality of products and services. For that reason, businesses are figuring out that offering only products and services is not enough to attract customers. Rather, they are relying on digital interfaces to offer their customers unique and impressive experiences. Second, digitization is enabling companies to deliver personalized and highly customized products and services. Businesses are capitalizing on new technologies to offer their customers the freedoms they seek based on the data that they collect. Third, because of the sharing economy, across the world and more particularly in North America, the concept of ownership is being replaced by access and utility [29]. More than 110 million people are participating in the collaborative economy in North America alone [26]. More and more, customers are attracted to businesses models based on sharing and access, convenience, and affordability, rather than ownership. As the prospects of sharing economy rise, businesses are facing new challenges to change the way they track and respond to customer expectations. Businesses collect and use data to create digitally enabled revenue models by tailoring products and services to their consumers' needs and preferences. Conversely, customers desire to take more control of their own product, service, or brand experience; they expect to have access to transparent information about the features of products and services. In the new age of consumption digitization, peer review and advocacy are gaining importance, and customers rely on peer recommendations to make their decisions [26]. Therefore, it is important for the businesses how to engage customers in the new digital channels not only to make short-term profits, but also to create lasting pleasant digital experiences. Many businesses, particularly those operating in traditional industries, are required to invest heavily in the digitization of their business processes to meet the lofty expectations of their customers.

Consumers' Attention as a Precious Commodity

Attention is defined as the allocation of mental resources to visible or conceptual objects and is considered key to marketing management [27]. Indeed, without attention, advertising has no impact on consumers. For that reason, advertising managers always seek to grab consumers' attention in order to convert it to purchase behavior. It is widely accepted that greater attention leads to higher advertising impact, and thus higher sales. Attention is a complex concept, but can be reduced to two major dimensions: intensity and duration. The intensity is a measure of the quality of attention during an interval, while the duration refers to its quantity [27]. In the past three decades, both the intensity and duration of consumers' attention have been declining. Based on a study conducted by Microsoft, since 2000, the average person's attention span has dropped from 12 seconds to only 8 seconds [28]. Our personal and social lives have been invaded by a plethora of audiovisual information coming from the new media, including the Internet, mobile devices, and traditional media such as radio, television, and newspapers. Most people find an advertising video of 52 seconds too long. The more we are exposed to information, the more we get distracted, and the more we lose our attention.

The success of some Internet platforms such as Twitter, Facebook, and Snapchat is based on quickly catching their consumers' attention by offering short-format content. For example, Snapchat is a highly popular platform among the young mobile-generation that is positioning itself by offering short and disposable contents. With over 10 billion daily video views, Snapchat hosts only videos that are 10 seconds or shorter [28]. Along with shortening attention spans, the quality of consumers' attention has been deteriorating in the past decades. Indeed, many indexes confirm that consumers have lost interest in the information content of the advertisement. Consumers do not feel the need of advertisement very much as they can obtain any piece of information on a company's products, prices, and technical features from a wide range of sources, including the company's website or from the peer evaluations. Webpages can be seen as replacements of advertisement that are available, reliable, and often more informative and more customized than advertisements. In short, we may suggest that consumers are attributing less attention to advertisement because of a wide range of factors. They are increasingly exposed to commercial messages, but they do not see any benefits in them as they have extensive information outlets at their disposal [27]. Facing the lack of customers' interest in the advertisement, businesses have reacted by increasing the volume of their advertisement, and by grating price promotions. These countermeasures have caused adverse effects on both current profits and future revenues and have resulted in the rising cost of buying customers' attention [27]. For example, it is suggested that the price of high-quality attention has risen as much as nine-fold in the last two decades [27]. This trend is expected to continue in the near future, and the market for consumer attention is supposed to become even more crowded and more competitive. As such, the customers' attention may be viewed as a precious commodity that should be managed judiciously. Considering the fierce competition for consumers' attention, marketing managers have to adapt the adequate advertising strategy to the level of attention in order to increase their advertisement campaign's success [27]. Marketing managers may use cautious advertising principles to buy customers' attention at a cheaper price. They may create advertisements that are effective even under low levels of attention. Finally, marketing managers may use advertisement content that causes higher levels of attention, so it can be more effectively converted into persuasion and purchase behavior [27].

References

[1] Kharas, H. 2010. *The Emerging Middle Class in Developing Countries.* Brookings Institution.

[2] Murphy, K.M., A. Shleifer, and R. Vishny. 1989. "Income Distribution, Market Size, and Industrialization." *The Quarterly Journal of Economics* 104, no. 3, pp. 537–64.

[3] Collier, P. 2007. "The Bottom Billion." *Economic Review-Deddington* 25, no. 1, p. 17.

[4] Kaufmann, D., A. Kraay, and M. Mastruzzi. 2009. *Governance Matters VIII: Aggregate and Individual Governance Indicators* 1996–2008. The World Bank.

[5] Kharas, H., and G. Gertz. 2010. *The New Global Middle Class: A Cross-Over from West to East*, 1–14. Wolfensohn Center for Development at Brookings.

[6] https://statista.com/statistics/225123/chinas-share-of-the-global-car-market/

[7] Yueh, L. 2013. "The Rise of the Global Middle Class." *BBC News*, June, 18.

[8] Dadush, U.B., and S. Ali. 2012. *In Search of the Global Middle Class: A New Index.* Carnegie Endowment for International Peace.

[9] United Nations, Department of Economic and Social Affairs, Population Division. "World Urbanization Prospects: The 2014 Revision."

[10] Henderson, J.W., and M. Castells. 1987. *Global Restructuring and Territorial Development.* Sage Publications Limited.

[11] United Nations, Department of Economic and Social Affairs, Population Division. 2014. "World Urbanization Prospects: The 2014 Revision, Highlights (ST/ESA/SER.A/352)."

[12] Bloom, D.E. 2016. "Demographic Upheaval." *Finance and Development* 53, no. 1, pp. 6–11.

[13] Dicken, P. 2007. *Global Shift: Mapping the Changing Contours of the World Economy.* Sage Publications Ltd.

[14] Guadalupe, M., H. Li, and J. Wulf. 2013. "Who Lives in the C-Suite? Organizational Structure and the Division of Labor in Top Management." *Management Science* 60, no. 4, pp. 824–44.

[15] Winthrop, R., G. Bulloch, P. Bhatt, and A. Wood. 2015. "Development Goals in an Era of Demographic Change." *Global Monitoring Report*, 2016.

[16] The United Nations, Department of Economics and Social Affairs, http://un.org/en/development/desa/population/publications/factsheets/index.shtml

[17] Dobbs, R., J. Remes, J. Manyika, J.R. Woetzel, J. Perrey, G. Kelly, and H. Sharma. 2016. *Urban World: The Global Consumers to Watch.* McKinsey Global Institute.

[18] Khanna, P. 2016. *Connectography: Mapping the Future of Global Civilization.* Random House.

[19] Marchese, K., and B. Lam. 2014. *Anticipatory Supply Chains Business Trends 2014: Navigating the Next Wave of Globalization.*

[20] Dediu, H. 2012. "When Will Smartphones Reach Saturation in the US?" Retrieved from http://asymco.com/2012/04/11/when-will-smartphones-reach-saturation-in-the-us/

[21] Goyal, T. 2001. "Shortening Product Life Cycles?" *Electronic News (North America)* 47, no. 16, p. 46.

[22] Geyer, R., L.N. Van Wassenhove, and A. Atasu. 2007. "The Economics of Remanufacturing Under Limited Component Durability and Finite Product Life Cycles." *Management Science* 53, no. 1, pp. 88–100.

[23] Goldman, A. 1982. "Short Product Life Cycles: Implications for the Marketing Activities of Small High-Technology Companies." *R & D Management* 12, no. 2, pp. 81–90.

[24] https://mckinsey.com/business-functions/marketing-and-sales/our-insights/digitizing-the-consumer-decision-journey

[25] Accenture. 2015. *Digital Transformation in the Age of the Customer: A Spotlight on B2C.* https://accenture.com/_acnmedia/Accenture/Conversion-Assets/DotCom/Documents/Global/PDF/Digital_2/Accenture-Digital-Transformation-B2C-spotlight.pdf

[26] Pilkington, M. 2016. "11 Blockchain Technology: Principles and Applications." *Research Handbook on Digital Transformations*, p. 225.

[27] Teixeira, T.S. 2014. *The Rising Cost of Consumer Attention: Why You Should Care, and What You Can do About It.*

[28] Lindner, E. 2012. "A Dignity Economy: Creating an Economy that Serves Human Dignity and Preserves Our Planet." *Dignity Press*, https://adweek.com/digital/john-stevens-guest-post-decreasing-attention-spans/

[29] https://mckinsey.com/business-functions/digital-mckinsey/our-insights/accelerating-the-digitization-of-business-processes

CHAPTER 9

Labor, Work Organization, and Education

1. The Slowdown in Labor Growth and Aging Workforce in the United States
2. Growing Importance of Cognitive Skills and Education Attainment
3. The Move Toward a Flattened, Fluid, and Flexible Organization of Work
4. Growing Diversity of the Workforce
5. Automation is Expected to Displace a Huge Number of Jobs in the Short-and Mid-Term

The Slowdown in Labor Growth and Aging Workforce in the United States

Over the course of the next decades, the world's population will be aging rapidly across the globe, particularly in developed countries. Currently, there are around 962 million people aged 60 years or over in the world, comprising 13 percent of the global population and growing at a rate of about 3 percent per year [1]. By 2050, half of the global population will reside in countries where at least 20 percent of the inhabitants are aged 60 years or over [2]. In the United States, the pace of aging is so significant that, by 2050, the number of Americans aged 65 years and more will reach 90 million [3]. As a result, in the next few decades, we expect a general trend toward the aging workforce and slower labor growth across the United States. Nevertheless, the aging population and slow labor growth problem are much more notable in China, Japan, and many other European countries such as Italy and Germany. In the United States, the workforce growth has declined continually from 2.6 percent in the 1970s to 1.6 percent during the 1980s and 1.1 percent in the 1990s, despite immigration and higher participation of women in the workforce. In the past three decades, the increase in the labor force has been boosted mainly by progressively higher labor force participation by women and large inflows of immigrants. Since the 2000s, the female workforce participation rate has been approaching that of men. Therefore, the decline in the workforce growth is expected to be very significant in the next coming years. By 2025, the rate of workforce growth may decline to as low as 0.3 or 0.4 percent per year [4]. Because of the combined effects of the aging population and slower workforce growth, some businesses may encounter difficulty in finding and recruiting qualified workers, especially in periods of faster economic growth [5]. The reliance of businesses on women and migrants will lead to the formation of a balanced workforce marked by different age cohorts, genders, and visible minorities. An aging workforce necessitates substantial changes to the workplace regulations and atmosphere because older workers have special needs. For example, workers aged 65 years and older have been shown to experience higher rates of permanent disabilities and workplace fatalities than their younger counterparts in the same industries and occupations.

Growing Importance of Cognitive Skills and Education Attainment

The transition from an industrial to a knowledge-based economy is expected to accelerate in the next decades. The global decline in the manufacturing sector, combined with automation technologies, will reduce the demand for labor-intensive and entry-level jobs and will boost job creation in technology, engineering, and computer science [6]. Consequently, the demand for highly skilled and educated workers will continue to accelerate. These trends imply that the economies that can train and maintain a high-skilled workforce are expected to outperform. Businesses will continue to look for the technical workforce capable of operating computer systems, developing and installing software, and managing networks. Organizations, whether for-profit or non-profit, are expected to favor workers with high-level cognitive skills such as abstract reasoning, problem-solving, communication, and collaboration. Furthermore, those workers who can interact in a global marketplace, participate in cross-national teams, and collaborate in diverse cultural and linguistic settings will have higher chances of recruitment and achievement. The mounting demand has been driving up the salary premium paid to workers with higher skills and education levels since the late 1990s. Closely associated with the demand for a highly skilled workforce is the educational attainment measured as years of schooling. Between 1973 and 2001, the wage premium for a college degree compared with a high school diploma increased 30 percent from 46 percent to 76 percent [5]. For that reason, the level of education attainment has been increasing in most of the developed and developing economies [7]. In the United States, college graduation rates among young white men and women have been rising, but a substantial fraction of African–Americans and Hispanics workers are still lagging behind. Compared to other developed nations, the U.S. students' scores are ranked about the average, despite greater public and private expenditures on education. For example, schooling expenditures amounted to 2.3 percent of the gross domestic product (GDP) in the United States versus 1.9 percent of the GDP in Canada, and around 1 percent of the GDP in other G8 countries [8]. The relatively low ranking of the U.S. students could be because of widespread educational, cognitive, and social disparities among American students. Considering the scale of upcoming technological disruptions, we may expect an extraordinary rate of change in the core curriculum contents of many academic fields. Based on some estimates, nearly 50 percent of subject knowledge acquired during the first year of a four-year technical degree could be outdated by the time students graduate [6]. Technological advances increase the demand for a more skilled workforce, but at the same time, new technologies provide immense opportunities to support the workers' education and training. The knowledge economy necessitates continuous learning and training throughout the working life, and many organizations are gradually relying on technology and the use of computers and other information technologies to enhance their workers' skills. The technology-mediated learning has the potential to offer efficient, individualized, and affordable education to a large number of students and employees and is becoming an integral part of workforce training.

The Move Toward Flattened, Fluid, and Flexible Organizations of Work

Technological forces and their subsequent social transformations are making organizations less vertical, more decentralized, and more specialized. To adapt themselves to the new conditions, the organizations shift from the rigid pyramidal structures to participatory management. The increasing importance of knowledge and intellectual property is pushing many organizations to empower their employees at all the organizational levels [9]. Under the new circumstances, offering employees with higher levels of authority and decision-making can result in higher levels of productivity. More specialization is pushing many organizations to rely more and more on outsourcing, even for crucial activities such as industrial design, manufacturing processes, business processing tasks, and human resources. Globalization is creating opportunities for outsourcing on a global scale, and organizations will continue to exploit the cost advantages across borders. In search of efficiency, organizations may scatter their value chain activities across the globe or break up their structures into semi-autonomous units. The new telecommunication technologies provide opportunities for firms to manage or coordinate their decentralized structures. Consistent with these transformations, there will be an increase in the portion of workers in flexible arrangements such as self-employment, contract work, temporary help, and lease agreements. Undeniably, transient work arrangements are expected to become more widespread in the face of rapid technological change and competitive market pressures [10]. The new forms of organizations could be based on electronically connected networks of contractors, freelancers, and semi-autonomous entities. The focus of work is gradually shifting from the solid organizational structures to flexible and project-based operations. Under the fierce competition from globalization and outsourcing, employers are increasingly turning to part-time, contingent, and contract workers to meet their business goals. According to one estimate, the freelance workforce may grow to 40 percent of the U.S. workforce or nearly 60 million workers by 2020 [11]. Those employees who stay with their organizations may have to work under part-time and other flexible work arrangements [12]. These transformations may have significant implications for the current employment laws and regulations, tax systems, employees' benefits such as healthcare, life or disability insurance, and pensions that are generally defined for regular and traditional organizations [13]. Because of all these socio-economic transformations, the organization of work is moving toward a flattened, fluid, and flexible configuration [14].

In tandem with the move toward a flexible organization of work, innovative technologies are changing the very concept of the workplace. Unlike the traditional workplace, the new workplace arrangements are not reliant on a physical space. While many salary jobs, particularly those involving manufacturing, will continue to be tied to a designated physical space, a growing portion of the workforce will move toward distance work when tasks can be done off-site [15]. These work arrangements are beneficial as teleworking allows employers to accommodate the needs of workers who care for children at home or for a sick family member. The new concept of workplace implies that a geographic place gradually may become even less relevant, and cities may lose their importance as the centers of economic activity [16]. For instance, high-tech centers are forming on the fringes of major metropolitan areas or in such smaller urban areas as Austin, Texas, and Raleigh, North Carolina [5]. In other words, technology is flattening the structure of geographic space into smaller horizontal regions with specialized agglomeration.

The flexibility and fluidity of work arrangements do not equate with the employee's freedom, as many employers can rely on new data-driven tools to control and monitor their off-site workers. For example, the software firm Sociometrics Solutions has developed badges that can track tone, mood, and stress during employee conversations [17]. Obviously, wearing a mood-sensing badge makes monitoring obvious to workers, but there are other data-driven techniques that can be used covertly by employers. Future analytics tools may use Big Data approaches to match jobs and workers and appraise or manage them more effectively. There are some software and tools that can be used across social media and other online sources to identify potentially qualified workers [18]. In a conventional way, workers have to demonstrate their skills and capabilities during the job interview by relying on their credentials, degrees, and other pieces. In the future, some new evaluation metrics will enable employers to measure the candidates' skills much more accurately. These kinds of workforce analytics need ethical considerations to secure workers' privacy and to protect them from potential employment discrimination [17].

Growing Diversity of the Workforce

In the past decades, immigration has substantially influenced the U.S. population and workforce composition. While relative to the population size, immigration was biggest in the early part of the 20th century, in the past three decades, the absolute number of immigrants has been the largest. According to the Bureau of Labor Statistics, in 2017, there were 27.4 million foreign-born persons in the U.S. labor force, comprising 17.1 percent of the total workforce. Hispanics and Asians, respectively, accounted for 47.9 and 25.2 percent of the foreign-born labor force in 2017. That is the highest proportion in records going back to 1996 when immigrants accounted for just 10.8 percent of the workforce [19]. Hispanics and Asians are the fastest growing racial and ethnic groups in the population. The number of Hispanics in the American workforce is expected to grow because of high birth rates, as well as ongoing immigration. Consistent with the current trends, much of the growth in the U.S. workforce will be fueled by immigration and the growing work participation of socio-ethnic minorities. The population aging and higher participation of women in the workforce are other emerging trends that will affect the composition of the workforce. The American labor force is becoming more balanced with regard to genders as the labor force participation for women and men are, respectively, increasing and declining. Therefore, the U.S. workforce is expected to become older, more feminine, and more ethnic-racially diverse in the next three decades.

Automation Is Expected to Displace a Huge Number of Jobs in the Short- and Mid-Term

Automation is the outcome of various technologies such as artificial intelligence, digitization, robotics, and connectivity and is expected to involve massive social and economic disruption. The upcoming revolution will enable the computerization of a wide range of simple and complex, cognitive and physical, or routine and changing tasks. Automation remains an emerging and complex phenomenon and is almost impossible to predict its consequences. Generally, there are two major views on the consequences of automation for the future of work. The optimistic view is to see automation as the source of entirely new industries that can attract the displaced workers. The pessimistic view implies that automation will eliminate a large number of jobs permanently, but will not create opportunities for the displaced or unemployed workers. The optimistic view relies on the premise that human and machine will develop a collaborative relation, so work will be done by both humans and automated systems. The proponents of this perspective argue that human and machine collaboration will lead to highly positive outcomes for the economy. The more meaningful and rewarding tasks will be done by human beings, while menial and routine tasks are done by machines. Consequently, humans will increasingly be supported by automation in the workplace, improving productivity and developing new opportunities. Accordingly, human–machine cooperation may lead to the creation of new kinds of jobs because humans will need to develop new skills and ways of thinking in order to collaborate with automated systems. In other words, in the long term, automation will not reduce the amount of work available to workers, but rather will reorder it. In the short term, automation may reduce the amount of work available to human workers, as it takes time for the economic systems to adapt to new technologies. The risk of job elimination due to automation is particularly serious in the case of lower-skill and lower entry positions that are characterized by low education attainment [17]. The other perspective about automation is more pessimistic and involves a general take over by machines that permanently eliminates a large number of jobs. The advocates of this perspective forecast that automation will reduce the need for physical and mental labor in the 21st century and will replace millions of workers from all sectors. The important point is that the disruption from automation will be so pervasive and permanent that new jobs will not suffice to replace the lost jobs. Accordingly, the automation process is considered as a continuous phenomenon that will ultimately move up the skill ladder by eliminating a large number of middle- to high-skill jobs in various sectors and industries [17].

Whether we subscribe to the optimistic or pessimistic perspective, it is credible to say that, in the short- and mid-term, the automation process is expected to significantly affect the labor market and eliminate a large number of jobs. The disagreement between the optimists and pessimists is essentially about the long-term outcomes. Therefore, it is crucial to identify effective ways to manage automation's impacts on workers' lives. The effects of automation will be particularly painful for the senior workers who are in the last stages of their careers and are either reluctant to or incapable of upgrading their professional skills.

References

[1]   United Nations, Department of Economic and Social Affairs, Population Division. "World Urbanization Prospects: The 2017 Revision."

[2]   Nations, U. 2013. "World Population Aging 2013." *Department of Economic and Social Affairs PD.*

[3]   Lam, D. 2011. "How the World Survived the Population Bomb: Lessons from 50 Years of Extraordinary Demographic History." *Demography* 48, no. 4, pp. 1231–62.

[4]   Fullerton, H.N., and M. Toossi. November 2001. "Labor Force Projections to 2010: Steady Growth and Changing Composition." *Monthly Labor Review*, pp. 21–38.

[5]   Karoly, L.A., and C.W. Panis. 2004. *The 21st Century at Work: Forces Shaping the Future Workforce and Workplace in the United States*, 64 vols. Rand Corporation.

[6]   World Economic Forum. January 2016. "The Future of Jobs: Employment, Skills and Workforce Strategy for the Fourth Industrial Revolution." In *World Economic Forum.*

[7]   Day, J.C., and K. Bauman. 2000. "Have We Reached the Top?: Educational Attainment Projections of the US Population." *Population Division.* US Census Bureau.

[8]   Organisation for Economic Co-operation and Development (OECD). 2001. *Education at a Glance.* Paris: OECD.

[9]   Zack, M.H. 2003. "Rethinking the Knowledge-Based Organization." *MIT Sloan Management Review* 44, no. 4, pp. 67–72.

[10] Waddoups, C.J. 2016. "Did Employers in the United States Back Away from Skills Training During the Early 2000s?" *ILR Review* 69, no. 2, pp. 405–34.

[11] Neuner, J. 2013. "40% of America's Workforce Will Be Freelancers by 2020." *Quartz*, March 20, http://qz.com/65279/40-of-americas-workforce-will-be-freelancers-by-2020

[12] Kantor, J. 2014. "Working Anything but 9 to 5." *New York Times*, August 13, nytimes.com/interactive/2014/08/13/us/starbucks-workers-scheduling-hours.html

[13] Thomas, W.M., and J.L. Robert. 1998. "The Dawn of the E-Lance Economy." *Harvard Business Review*, pp. 145–52.

[14] Anton, P.S., R. Silberglitt, and J. Schneider. 2001. "The Global Technology Revolution: bio/nano/Materials Trends and their Synergies with Information Technology by 2015." *Rand Corporation*.

[15] Hecker, D.E. November 2001. "Occupational Employment Projections to 2010." *Monthly Labor Review* 124, no. 11, pp. 57–84.

[16] Kotkin, J., and F.F. Siegel. 2000. *Digital Geography: The Remaking of City and Countryside in the New Economy*. Indianapolis, Ind: The Hudson Institute.

[17] Foresight Alliance LLC. 2016. "The Futures of Work." http://foresightalliance.com/wp-content/uploads/2010/03/The-Futures-of-Work-1.12.2016.pdf

[18] Richtel, M. 2013. "How Big Data Is Playing Recruiter for Specialized Workers." *New York Times*, April 27, www.nytimes.com/2013/04/28/technology/how-big-data-is-playing-recruiter-for-specialized-workers.html

[19] https://bls.gov/news.release/pdf/forbrn.pdf

PART III

Innovation and Technology

CHAPTER 10

Innovation and Research

1. The Shifting Landscape of Global Innovation
2. The Dependence of Innovation on Higher Education and Immigration
3. The Increasing Importance of Corporate Innovation
4. Frugal and Reverse Innovation Models
5. Innovation as Competitive Advantage
6. The Global Map of Innovation

The Shifting Landscape of Global Innovation

The global investment in research and development has been rising fast across the world and has reached one trillion U.S. dollars in 2015. The Group of Seven (G7) consisting of Canada, France, Germany, Italy, Japan, the United Kingdom, and the United States account for more than 615 billion U.S. dollars of this investment in research and development. The United States with 325 billion U.S. dollars and Japan with 123 billion U.S. dollars are still front-runners in all areas of innovation investment [1]. Nevertheless, consistent with other changes on the world stage, the landscape of global innovation is rapidly undergoing significant transformations. The shares of the United States and Japan in the global research and development spending have declined since the late-1990s, because of gains in China and other growth markets in Asia. In the past decade, Asia has surpassed the European Union in the research and development investment, and if the trend maintains, Asia could overtake the United States in a near future (see Figures 10.1 and 10.2). Multiple indicators reveal that the G7 countries are facing fierce rivalry from many emerging countries, particularly from China. As a matter of fact, the research and development spending is growing much faster in Asian countries than in G7 countries [1]. For example, in the past decade, the research and

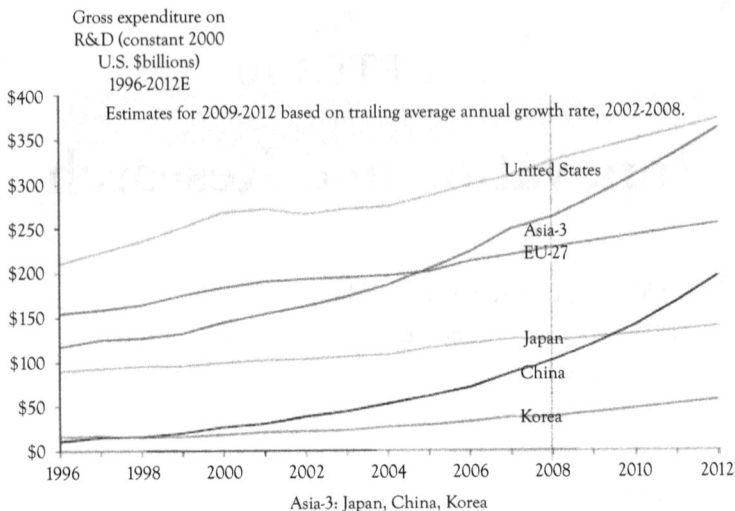

Figure 10.1 **Steady rise in global research and development investment (Asia outspends Europe, continues to converge to U.S. levels)**

Source: [2].

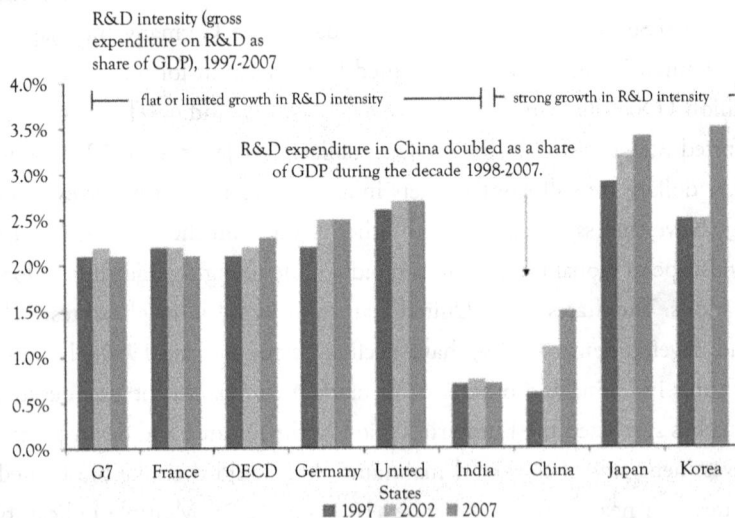

Figure 10.2 **Greatest research and development intensity gains are in Asia**

Source: OECD [2].

development spending has grown more than 20 percent per year in China and more than 8 percent per year in Korea. For the same period, the growth in the research and development investment has been hovering around 3 percent in G7 countries. Comparing the research and development spending to the gross domestic product (GDP) (measuring the R&D intensity) indicates that Asian countries such as China and South Korea have grown even at a faster pace than their Western counterparts have. As emerging countries continue to increase the size of their economies, they are motivated to increase their research and development budgets even more aggressively. China's government has the ambitious objective of spending 2.5 percent of the GDP on R&D by 2020, which means 300 billion U.S. dollars investment per year [1]. Obviously, the growth in research and development spending is only a part of the story, because, in addition to the increased spending, Asian countries are training a large number of researchers and scientists. In the past two decades, higher education has been growing fast outside the major developed countries. This has resulted in a steep rise in the number of researchers and innovators in developing countries. For example, the United States' share of the global university student population has declined from 20 percent in 1990 to less than 13 percent [1]. By contrast, for the same period, China's share of the global university students has more than doubled to 15 percent. Likewise, in recent years, Asian countries have become the origins of a growing number of patents and innovations, significantly improved high-tech trade balances, and experienced strong labor productivity growth. All these signs are indicative of a promising innovation in Asia.

The Dependence of Innovation on Higher Education and Immigration

Certainly, innovation is primarily about training qualified scientists and researchers who can conduct research and develop new products and services. The G7 advanced economies, particularly the United States, face major challenges in training qualified workers to stimulate or at least to maintain their technological edge. The basic data suggest that local students in G7 countries show insufficient interest in science and engineering education. For instance, science and engineering programs include less than 25 percent of the university degrees awarded in G7 countries, and only 15 percent of all new degrees awarded in the United States [1]. The United States enjoys an unmatched position in scientific innovation, and most of the top universities are located in the United States, but surprisingly, American secondary students are generally ranked lower in science and mathematics aptitude than their counterparts in other developed countries. The explanation is the American top universities and research institutions attract a large number of talented people from all over the globe. For example, most engineering PhD degrees at American universities are granted to people born abroad. The short supply of local scientists and researchers in the G7 countries and particularly in the United States is a major reason that businesses try to attract qualified immigrants. Consequently, a notable trend is that innovation in developed economies is becoming increasingly dependent on immigration. In the United States, more than 20 percent of the science and engineering workers are immigrants born in developing countries and high-skilled immigrants account for roughly a quarter of the U.S. patents [3]. In the United States, immigrants account for a disproportionate share of innovation superstars and are over-presented among most-cited authors, scholars, researchers, and among members of the National Academy of Sciences [4]. It has been found that American winners of the Nobel Prize are disproportionately from immigrants [5]. Other G7 countries are similar to the United States in this respect. For example, a study in Canada suggested that more than 35 percent of Canada Research Chairs are foreign-born, while immigrants are just one-fifth of the Canadian population [2]. In addition to talent and education, many immigrants are equipped with high levels of motivation, risk-taking capacity, and persistence that turn them to innovators par excellence. Inventors tend to be more mobile than the rest of the population. For example, 10 percent of the inventors worldwide showed a migratory background in 2005. The United States is the most popular destination for migrant inventors, hosting 57 percent of the world's inventors who reside outside their home countries. Almost 75 percent of the migrant inventors from low- and middle-income countries reside in the United States. China and India are the two largest origins of high-value migrants followed by Russia, Turkey, Iran, Romania, and Mexico

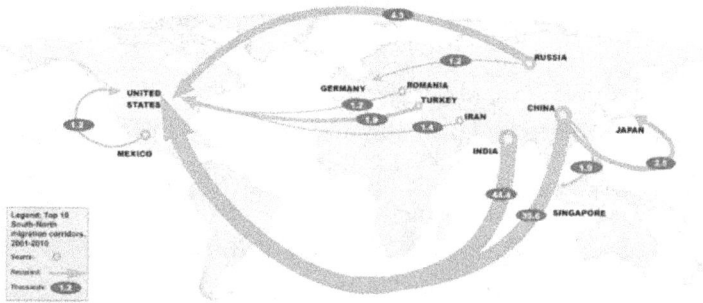

Figure 10.3 The origins of migrant inventors to the Unites States

Source: [6].

(see Figure 10.3). After the United States, Switzerland, Germany, and the United Kingdom are attractive destinations to inventors [6]. Among the larger European countries, the United Kingdom enjoys a relatively high share of immigrant inventors, while Germany, France, Italy, and Spain have a lower percentage of foreign-born citizens among their inventors. Considering the importance of immigration for innovation, public policies in G7 should aim at attracting highly skilled and educated migrant workers [1].

The Increasing Importance of Corporate Innovation

In the age of global capitalism, large multinational corporations are becoming the main producers, users, and disseminators of knowledge and innovation. For instance, multinational corporations are estimated to account for the majority of total global spending on research and development in the United States and Japan, as well as across many growth markets [7]. Based on some assessments, the research and development investment by American multinationals doubled between 1997 and 2007 [8]. In addition to huge investments in research and development, large multinationals play an important role in the dissemination of knowledge through their operations in different countries across the world. Multinationals apply the technical knowledge to build, introduce, and sell new products and processes across the globe. Multinationals and their affiliates are responsible for one-third of the world exports that ultimately circulate their innovative products throughout the world [9]. In addition to trade, multinational corporations disseminate innovation through competition and forward and backward integration strategies such as cross-national mergers and acquisitions. In order to maintain their competitive advantages, large multinationals continuously focus on research and development. Many of these multinationals see innovative advantages in acquiring small and entrepreneurial companies when building competencies themselves would simply take too long [10]. Because of concerns about the cost of innovation and infringement of intellectual property rights, many U.S.-based multinational corporations are focusing on incremental innovation or creative imitation. The global race toward innovation has led to a proliferation of innovation centers. Innovation centers represent enterprise investments that aim at understanding new market dynamics, acquiring new expertise and resources, and cooperating with entrepreneurs, startups, investors, academic institutions, and related ecosystems [11]. Innovation centers are located outside the traditional operational landscape with the goal of accelerating digital innovation, rethinking customer experience, improving operational efficiency, and testing new business models. Silicon Valley's reign as the epicenter of innovation hosts 65 innovation centers [11].

Frugal and Reverse Innovation Models

In tandem with the growth of emerging economies and their multinational corporations, the new tendencies such as frugal innovation and reverse innovation are becoming widespread. Frugal innovation is a broad concept that is described by characteristics such as affordability, low-cost manufacturing, low-cost materials, and focus on basic functionality [12]. Frugal innovation is essentially about the needs and circumstances of citizens in the developing economies in order to develop appropriate, adaptable, affordable, and accessible services and products [13]. Frugal innovation is encouraged by low-income consumers and resource scarcity [14]. Frugally innovative organizations rely on more cost-effective products, services, processes, and business models [15]. Simply put, frugal innovation is primarily the ability to create significantly more value by minimizing the use of resources such as energy, capital, and time [16].

Frugal innovation surmounts financial, technological, material or other resource constraints, in order to offer the final product, which is much cheaper than competitive alternatives. Frugal innovation is particularly popular and effective in the context of developing economies where a significant number of people live on low levels of income [17]. The mass markets in the bottom of the pyramid have attracted multinational companies from around the world to frugal innovation. While multinational companies from advanced economies initially aimed at exploiting the low-cost manufacturing in developing economies, they gradually created centers for investing in R&D in their host countries and took advantage of frugal innovation [18]. As an increasing number of multinational corporations from developed economies are targeting the low-income customer base in developing or low-income countries, the strategic importance of frugal innovation continues to grow. More recently, we have been witnessing imitations and innovations led by multinational corporations based in emerging or developing economies. Emerging markets multinationals are not big innovators; rather, they are recognized as imitators that duplicate intellectual property from their rivals in advanced economies and adapt it to local consumers. As emerging markets are maturing, they are keen on moving away from imitations to innovations. Features such as improvisation, adjustment to the local markets, and organizational novelty mark such innovations. These types of innovation are more adapted to developing economies' needs, constraints, culture, and customs. Because of shortages of capital, technology, and talent, the entrepreneurs in developing economies need to find solutions to their problems with rare resources. These frugal innovations are low-cost solutions for low-income customers. For example, much of Haier's success is attributed to developing products adapted to Chinese customers.

Some frugal innovations, labeled as reverse innovations, are exported from developing and low-income countries to developed and high-income economies. Frugal innovation involves designing solutions specifically for low-income market segments, but reverse innovation involves new products developed in emerging markets, which are then modified for sale in developed economies [19]. In other words, reverse innovation denotes low-cost innovations, which are first adopted in emerging economies and then *trickle up* to developed countries [20]. Reverse innovation is about developing new products in emerging markets first and modify them for sale in developed countries later. The reverse innovation has become an important part of the global innovation, implying that developing countries are not merely recipients of innovations from developed countries. Sometimes, the Western multinational corporations use the reverse innovation models in order to reduce their costs and enhance their competitiveness in their home countries. For instance, companies like Siemens and General Electric have been developing such unique products, which are developed specially for the emerging and developing countries consumers and also have potential to succeed in the developed markets [21].

Innovation as Competitive Advantage

Traditionally, countries and companies have been labeled competitive on the basis of their static comparative advantages, including natural and physical endowments, the cost of factors of production, or specific technological advantages. More recently, the competitiveness at the national and organizational levels is defined as a complex concept that depends on the capacity of continuous innovation, high skills, learning, efficient communications, transport infrastructures, and supportive environments [22]. In the rapidly changing global business context, firms have to constantly innovate to keep their competitive edge over their rivals. We may consider five areas of innovation, including generation of new or improved products, introduction of the new production process, development of new sales market, development of new supply market, and reorganization of the company [23]. Therefore, innovation includes the process of creating a new product or service, new technologic process, a new organization, and enhancement of existing product, technologic process, or organization [24]. The innovation process can be radical or incremental. A radical innovation is about developing products, processes, or services with unprecedented features, while incremental innovation involves improvements in cost or existing processes, products, and services [25]. Thus, innovation has many dimensions and goes beyond technological advances. For instance, innovation may include more efficient managerial techniques and flexible organizational models [25]. Many giant firms such as Dell, Uber, Amazon, and Netflix owe their success to innovative business models, rather than to their technological innovations. For example, Dell developed an innovative business model by subcontracting production to third parties, eliminating distributors, and selling directly to the final consumer. Likewise, Wal-Mart took advantage of an innovative business model by monitoring consumer demand and linking that information via central ordering directly to producers all around the world in order to eliminate intermediaries in production and distribution [8]. A company's innovative capacity is the result of relationships between its organizational culture, resources, competencies, and relationships with other organizations. The need for innovation is translated into higher investment in research and development and in the education and training programs. Currently, we are witnessing an extraordinary wave of acceleration in the creation and dissemination of knowledge. The lapses between basic scientific discovery and commercial application are declining fast and as a result, innovation is becoming a tough race [20].

The Global Map of Innovation

The Global Innovation Index report (2018) ranks more than 120 countries by relying on six key pillars, including infrastructure, human capital and research, institutions, market sophistication, business sophistication, knowledge and technology outputs, and creative outputs [27]. Based on this comprehensive approach, there are significant disparities across the world with regard to innovation [26]. North America, Europe, and South East Asia are ranked as the innovation leaders, while Latin America, Sub-Saharan Africa, and Central and Southern Asia are considered as the innovation laggards. In the 2018 Global Innovation Index report, the United States is placed at the 6th rank, which means a decline from 2017. Indeed, the United States has increased its innovation ranking since 2012, mainly because of the advancement in information technologies, Internet, and financial sector. In absolute terms, the United States is the top contributor in key innovation inputs and outputs, including investment in research and development, and second after China in the volume of researchers, patents, and scientific and technical publications. Canada, another North American economy, is ranked the 18th position overall, with advantages in ease of starting a business and venture capital deals.

The top 11 innovating economies are European, including Switzerland, the Netherlands, and Sweden. While the European Union is among the most innovative areas, there are significant levels of disparity among the European countries. For example, many European countries are included in the top 10, while some are in the top 30 and 40, or even in the top 50 [26]. All countries in South East Asia, East Asia, and Oceania region are ranked within the top 100 innovators. In this region, Singapore, the Republic of Korea, and Japan are ranked as highly innovative. Singapore keeps its first place in government effectiveness, regulatory quality, and foreign direct investment outflows. Japan ranks 1st in gross domestic expenditure on research and development financed by businesses. The Republic of Korea maintains its top rankings in patent applications by origin and various indicators measuring research and development efforts. In the Central and Southern Asia region, India, Iran, and Kazakhstan are on the top of the list. India is categorized as a low-income economy and ranks well in a number of important indicators, including productivity growth, exports of information, and communication technology and services. Considering its large and rapidly growing population, India could make a big difference to the global innovation landscape in a near future. Iran maintains the second place in the Central and Southern Asia region and earns top ranks in productivity growth and graduates in science and engineering. In the Northern Africa and Western Asia, Israel, Cyprus, and the United Arab Emirates are ranked at the top of the list. Israel leads in many indicators, including a number of researchers, research and development expenditures, venture capital deals, research talent in business enterprise, and exports of information and communications technology. In Latin America and the Caribbean, Chile, Costa Rica, Mexico, and Brazil rank high. Brazil, as the largest economy of the region, has strength in many areas, including research and development expenditures, high-tech net imports and exports, and quality of scientific publications and universities. In Sub-Saharan Africa, South Africa is on the top of the list followed by Mauritius and Kenya. South Africa shows strengths in its sophisticated market and business sector, access to credit, market capitalization, university and industry research collaborations, cluster development, and intellectual property payments.

Table 10.1 depicts the top innovative countries based on the Global Innovation Index [27]. It is noticeable that there is a positive link between innovation performance and an economy's level of development as measured by the GDP per capita. This means that high-income countries

Table 10.1 Global innovation index rankings

Country/Economy	Score (0–100)	Rank	Income	Rank	Region	Rank	Efficiency Ratio	Rank	Median: 0.61
Switzerland	68.40	1	HI	1	EUR	1	0.96	1	
Netherlands	63.32	2	HI	2	EUR	2	0.91	4	
Sweden	63.08	3	HI	3	EUR	3	0.82	10	
United Kingdom	60.13	4	HI	4	EUR	4	0.77	71	
Singapore	59.83	5	HI	5	SEAO	1	0.61	63	
United States of America	59.81	6	HI	6	NAC	1	0.76	22	
Finland	59.63	7	HI	7	EUR	5	0.76	24	
Denmark	58.39	8	HI	8	EUR	6	0.73	29	
Germany	58.03	9	HI	9	EUR	7	0.83	9	
Ireland	57.19	10	HI	10	EUR	8	0.81	13	
Israel	56.79	11	HI	11	NAWA	1	0.81	14	
Korea, Republic of	56.63	12	HI	12	SEAO	2	0.79	20	
Japan	54.95	13	HI	13	SEAO	3	0.68	44	
Hong Kong (China)	54.62	14	HI	14	SEAO	4	0.64	54	
Luxembourg	54.53	15	HI	15	EUR	9	0.94	2	
France	54.36	16	HI	16	EUR	10	0.72	32	
China	53.06	17	UM	1	SEAO	5	0.92	3	
Canada	52.98	18	HI	17	NAC	2	0.61	61	
Norway	52.63	19	HI	18	EUR	11	0.64	52	
Australia	51.98	20	HI	19	SEAO	6	0.58	76	
Austria	51.32	21	HI	20	EUR	12	0.64	53	
New Zealand	51.29	22	HI	21	SEAO	7	0.62	59	
Iceland	51.24	23	HI	22	EUR	13	0.76	23	
Estonia	50.51	24	HI	23	EUR	14	0.82	12	
Belgium	50.50	25	HI	24	EUR	15	0.70	38	
Malta	50.29	26	HI	25	EUR	16	0.84	7	
Czech Republic	48.75	27	HI	26	EUR	17	0.80	17	
Spain	48.68	28	HI	27	EUR	18	0.70	36	
Cyprus	47.83	29	HI	28	NAWA	2	0.79	18	
Slovenia	46.87	30	HI	29	EUR	19	0.74	77	
Italy	46.32	31	HI	30	EUR	20	0.70	35	
Portugal	45.71	32	HI	31	EUR	21	0.71	34	
Hungary	44.94	33	HI	32	EUR	22	0.84	8	
Latvia	43.18	34	HI	33	EUR	23	0.69	39	
Malaysia	43.16	35	UM	2	SEAO	8	0.66	48	
Slovakia	42.88	36	HI	34	EUR	24	0.74	28	
Bulgaria	42.65	37	UM	3	EUR	25	0.79	19	
United Arab Emirates	42.58	38	HI	35	NAWA	3	0.50	95	
Poland	41.67	39	HI	36	EUR	26	0.69	42	
Lithuania	41.19	40	HI	37	EUR	27	0.61	58	

Source: [27].

are more likely to innovate, especially when their economic structures, and thus their industry portfolios are more diverse. All countries, regardless of their level of development, are likely to be more innovative when they have a more diversified export portfolio. The other findings of the Global Innovation Index report show that a country's size or population is not correlated with the level of innovation. Indeed, some small countries such as Switzerland, the Netherlands, Sweden, and Singapore are ranked among the top innovative nations [26]. According to the Global Innovation Index report (2018), a number of emerging economies are likely to continue their ascendency in the innovation rankings. China's ranking has been improving in the past decade, and the country is already among the top 25 innovative nations. Other countries, including India, Iran, Mexico, Thailand, and Vietnam, are consistently climbing in the rankings of the most innovative countries [27].

References

[1]   Gilman, D. 2010. *The New Geography of Global Innovation*. Global Markets Institute of Goldman Sachs.

[2]   The Conference Board of Canada. 2015. "Immigrants Make Significant Contributions to Innovation." https://www.conferenceboard.ca/?gclid= EAIaIQobChMIh561rpGq4AIVS5yzCh3KgQKTEAAYASAAEgIb UvD_BwE&gclsrc=aw.ds

[3]   Kerr, W.R. 2008. "Ethnic Scientific Communities and International Technology Diffusion." *The Review of Economics and Statistics* 90, no. 3, pp. 518–37.

[4]   Kerr, W.R. 2015. "International Migration and US Innovation: Insights from the US Experience." In *Routledge Handbook of Immigration and Refugee Studies*, 106–11. Routledge.

[5]   Hunt, J. 2012. *Does the United States Admit the Best and Brightest Computer and Engineering Workers*. Rutgers University working paper.

[6]   Fink, C., E. Miguelez, and J. Raffo. 2013. *The Global Race for Inventors*. Forthcoming as a WIPO Economic Research Working Paper.

[7]   Berger, S. 2006. *How We Compete: What Companies Around the World are Doing to Make it in Today's Global Economy*. New York, NY: Random House.

[8]   Dahlman, C. 2007. "Technology, Globalization, and International Competitiveness: Challenges for Developing Countries." *Asdf*, p. 29.

[9]   Kaplinsky, R. 2005. *Globalization, Poverty, and Inequality*. Cambridge: Polity Press.

[10] Brondoni, S.M. 2014. "Innovation and Imitation for Global Competitive Strategies." The Corporation Development Models of US, Japan, Korea, and Taiwan. Symphonya. *Emerging Issues in Management* 1, pp. 12–27.

[11] Garrity, T.F. March 2009. "Innovation and Trends for Future Electric Power Systems." In *Power Systems Conference*. PSC'09, 1–8. IEEE.

[12] Hossain, M., H. Simula, and M. Halme. 2016. "Can Frugal Go Global? Diffusion Patterns of Frugal Innovations." *Technology in Society* 46, pp. 132–39.

[13] Basu, R.R., P.M. Banerjee, and E.G. Sweeny. 2013. "Frugal Innovation: Core Competencies to Address Global Sustainability." *Journal of Management for Global Sustainability* 2, pp. 63–82.

[14] Sharma, A., and G.R. Iyer. 2012. "Resource-Constrained Product Development: Implications for Green Marketing and Green Supply Chains." *Industrial Marketing Management* 41, no. 4, pp. 599–608

[15] Hossain, M. 2015. "Frugal and Reverse Innovations: What, Where and Why?" *Clarifying the Concepts and Creating a Research Agenda*.

[16] Radjou, N., and J. Prabhu. 2015. "Frugal Innovation: How to do More with Less." *The Economist*.

[17] Walsh, J.P., J.C. Kress, and K.W. Beyerchen. 2005. "CK Prahalad: The Fortune at the Bottom of the Pyramid: Eradicating Poverty through Profits." *Administrative Science Quarterly* 50, no. 3, p. 473.

[18] Singhal, V. 2011. "The Impact of Emerging Economies Innovative New Models of Global Growth and Vitality are Emerging." *Visions* 35, no. 2, pp. 12–14.

[19] Nunes, P.F., and T. Breene. 2011. *Jumping the S-curve: How to Beat the Growth Cycle, Get on Top, and Stay There*. Harvard Business Press.

[20] Govindarajan, V., and C. Trimble. 2009. "How GE Is Disrupting Itself (How General Electric has Switched to Selling Products Originally Aimed at Developing Country Markets to the USA)." *How GE is Disrupting Itself*, eds. J.R. Immelt, V. Govindarajan and C. Trimble. *Harvard Business Review* 87, no. 10, pp. 56–65.

[21] Agarwal, N., and A. Brem. June 2012. "Frugal and Reverse Innovation-Literature Overview and Case Study Insights from a German MNC in India and China." In *Engineering, Technology and Innovation (ICE), 2012 18th International ICE Conference on*, 1–11. IEEE.

[22] Dahlman, C.J., and J.E. Aubert. 2001. *China and the Knowledge Economy: Seizing the 21st Century*. Washington, DC: World Bank.

[23] Reguia, C. 2014. "Product Innovation and the Competitive Advantage." *European Scientific Journal, ESJ* 10, no. 10.

[24] Ramadani, V., and S. Gerguri. 2011. *Theoretical Framework of Innovation: Competitiveness and Innovation Program in Macedonia*.

[25] Sh, G., G. Rexhepi, and V. Ramadani. 2013. "Innovation Strategies and Competitive Advantage." *Modern Economy: Challenges, Trends, Prospects* 8, p. 1.

[26] Asheim, B.T., and M.S. Gertler. 2005. "The Geography of Innovation: Regional Innovation Systems." In *The Oxford Handbook of Innovation*.

[27] Dutta, S., R.E. Reynoso, A. Garanasvili, K. Saxena, B. Lanvin, S. Wunsch-Vincent, and F. Guadagno. 2018. "The Global Innovation Index 2018: Energizing The World with Innovation." *Global Innovation Index 2018*, p. 1.

CHAPTER 11

Emerging Technologies

1. Automation and Robotics
   Augmented Intelligence
   Autonomous Vehicles
   Drones and Unmanned Aerial Vehicles

2. Data and Connectivity
   5G Mobile Internet and the Internet of Things
   Blockchain
   Bluetooth 5.0 and Li-Fi
   Li-Fi
   Quantum Computing
   Smart Dust

3. Interfaces and Visualization
   Deep Mapping
   Mixed Reality
   Multi-Sensory Interfaces

4. Materials
   Nanomaterials
   Programmable Materials
   Bio-Based Materials

5. Energy and Resources
   Foam Batteries
   Fusion Reactors
   Transparent Solar Panels
   Pollution Digesters

Automation and Robotics

Augmented Intelligence

Augmented intelligence involves the use of intelligent tools by human beings in order to enhance their intellectual and cognitive capacities [1]. Augmented intelligence systems rely on machine learning to extend human cognitive abilities such as the brain's capacity to calculate, assess, prioritize, and analyze information. Augmented Intelligence systems use natural language processing, spatial navigation, machine vision, logical reasoning, and pattern recognition [1]. In other words, augmented intelligence systems help connect people and computers to jointly analyze, interpret, and process the fast-changing big data in real time. While most artificial intelligence methods focus on replacing humans, augmented intelligence aims at creating collaboration between machines and humans. The augmented intelligence systems are characterized by five major abilities: (1) understanding, they derive meaning from all forms of multi-structured data and user interactions, (2) interpreting, they represent the meaning in a deterministic and probabilistic knowledge graph based on declared, observed, and inferred entities, events, and relationships, (3) reasoning, they reason over the domain-optimized interpretation in business and user context to come up with personalized advice with supporting evidence, (4) learning, they learn continuously based on real-time and historical data, user, and system interactions, and (5) assuring, they ensure ongoing compliance and governance for responsible and risk-managed use of cognitive services [1]. By using these capacities, augmented intelligence will assist users to make more informed and faster decisions in a wide range of areas, including finance, investment, healthcare, manufacturing, retail, travel and tourism, energy, and agriculture. Augmented intelligence systems can be used by businesses that are facing fast-changing customer behavior, strict security and regulatory requirements. For instance, augmented intelligence may help patients with chronic diseases get personalized care and avoid medical errors. Augmented intelligence systems can analyze an individual's environment and lifestyle patterns to deliver targeted health-related recommendations. Likewise, financial planners can use augmented intelligence systems to offer personalized financial services to their clients. Augmented intelligence systems can help shoppers in their shopping experience depending on the context, occasion, and location of their purchase [1].

Autonomous Vehicles

In the past two decades, advances in multiple technologies such as robotics, navigation, sensing, computer vision, and high-performance computing have revived interest in autonomous vehicles. Autonomous vehicles are being developed along two streams: (1) vehicle automation, which consists of technologies concerning automation of vehicle control functions without direct driver inputs, and (2) vehicle connectivity, which consists of different vehicular communication technologies such as vehicle-to-vehicle, vehicle-to-infrastructure, and vehicle-to-personal device communication [2]. Indeed, vehicle automation is part of a much larger revolution in automation and connectivity, as multiple technologies are combined to sense and manipulate the physical environment [3].

The National Highway Traffic Safety Administration (NHTSA) proposed a five-level conceptualization of the automated vehicles as the following [4]

Level 0: No automation, the human driver is in complete control of all functions of the car.

Level 1: Driver assistance, the vehicle can assist the driver or take control of either the vehicle's speed or its lane position.

Level 2: More than one function is automated at the same time, but the driver must remain constantly attentive.

Level 3: Limited self-driving, the driving functions are sufficiently automated that the driver can safely engage in other activities.

Level 4: Full self-driving under certain conditions.

Level 5: Full self-driving under all conditions: the vehicle can operate without a human driver or occupants.

A future with autonomous motor vehicles is not very far away, as currently, various models of autonomous vehicles are being tested in research facilities and on public roads. A growing number of carmakers are showing interest in autonomous vehicles, including Audi, BMW, Ford, GM,

Mercedes-Benz, Nissan, Toyota, Volkswagen, Volvo, Tesla, and Local Motors. Even technology companies such as Apple, Google, and Uber are investing in autonomous vehicles technology [2]. There is extensive agreement that Levels 3–5 of automated vehicles will be commercially available to some buyers within five years or even as early as 2020. In 2016, Ford announced its plans to have a high-volume, fully autonomous SAE Level 4 vehicle in commercial operation in 2021 in a ride-hailing or ride-sharing service [5]. Autonomous vehicles will be probably available for sale across the country in a few years, but all vehicles on the road will not be autonomous and conventional driving will continue to exist for a long time [4]. Most experts believe that Level 4 or 5 of autonomous vehicles will be widely commercialized sometime after 2025–2040 [4]. According to a recent study, the Netherlands, Singapore, the United States, Sweden, and the United Kingdom are ranked as the most prepared countries for the commercialization and the widespread use of autonomous vehicles with regard to policy and legislation, technology, infrastructure, and consumer acceptance [6].

The commercialization of autonomous vehicles will have substantial implications for many aspects of our lives including transportation, jobs, urban planning and infrastructure, economic models, and more obviously for roadway rules and regulations. Autonomous vehicles are expected to reduce human error on roadways, improve capacity on the roadways, and increase the utilization of travel time [7]. The market for liability coverage may be impacted significantly for manufacturers, owners, and operators [8]. Autonomous cars are expected to significantly reduce the cost of congestion because drivers could engage in alternative activities. Autonomous vehicles could restructure transportation models that are based on car ownership. Furthermore, autonomous vehicles can increase the mobility of young people, the elderly, the disabled, and other communities underserved by traditional personal and public transportation systems [7]. The commercialization of autonomous cars could lead to more dispersed and low-density patterns of land use surrounding metropolitan regions [9]. Currently, a large portion of space in metropolitan regions is devoted to parking. Naturally, the use of autonomous vehicles and sharing programs necessitate fewer parking spaces, and thus could revolutionize the land use in metropolitan areas. The overall effect of autonomous vehicles on energy and pollution is indeterminate, but it is widely expected that autonomous vehicles will reduce energy use and pollution. Autonomous vehicles require adapted infrastructure, pavements, traffic signals, signs, and street markings. Moreover, the autonomous vehicle needs the installation of various types of sensors and communications technology to allow vehicles to travel more efficiently [10]. Buildings will need to be located and designed to facilitate both pedestrians and autonomous deliveries. The commercialization of the autonomous vehicle technology involves some important impacts on the transportation industry and associated sectors. For instance, truck, bus, taxi, and delivery vehicles are expected to undergo major transformations. Cab and truck drivers and mechanics may lose their jobs, and the revenues derived from selling or renting parking spots may decline or disappear. Likewise, all those workers and institutions involved in car maintenance and insurance may be disrupted [9].

Drones and Unmanned Aerial Vehicles

The U.S. Department of Transportation estimates that the number of drones and unmanned aerial vehicles operations will exceed that of regular or manned aircraft operations by 2035 [11]. The rising popularity of drones and unmanned aerial vehicles is the result of recent developments in a wide range of technologies, including microprocessors, GPS, sensors, batteries, motors, lightweight structural materials, and advanced manufacturing techniques. Drones can be used in many sectors, including agriculture, energy, public safety, security, military, e-commerce, delivery, and transport. In the military sector and defense, drones are already employed, and their application will continue to increase in the next several years. Drones can be used in precision agriculture to enhance farms' productivity. In the energy sector, drones may reduce various risks to personnel performing hazardous tasks, or the risks to the environment and assets. Furthermore, they can be used in inspecting industrial infrastructure, oil refineries, pipelines, tanks, and power lines. In public safety and security, drones can play an essential role by facilitating the assessment and management of hazardous situations. In e-commerce and delivery, the drone may be used to deliver packages and supply materials more efficiently and more quickly. Most of all, drones can replace the present aircraft, railways, buses, and taxis by providing safe, reliable, and fast mobility. Autonomous drones can be used as a mode of transport to carry individuals or small groups of passengers to a destination. Currently, different prototypes are in development for use, particularly in high-density urban environments. Passenger drone is a prototype that is slightly larger than a small car and can change the traditional means of commuter transportation by flying at a speed of 50 miles per hour [12]. Public acceptance for flights with automated drones will require substantial improvements in other technologies such as connectivity and autonomy in ground vehicles, aerial transport and the design of buildings, public spaces and power systems, as well as transport infrastructure. Dubai has already begun trials of a passenger drone service. The advent of partial and fully autonomous flying vehicles will be sometime after 2025 [13]. Drones will bring about new forms of air traffic, especially at very low levels of airspace with high demand in densely populated areas. The implications of such air traffic will be significant particularly in urban centers.

Data and Connectivity

5G Mobile Internet and the Internet of Things

As the volume of data is growing exponentially, the next generation of the mobile Internet or 5G is expected to handle huge amounts of data, connect more devices, reduce latency, and provide increased network reliability. The 5G networks have a speed of 10 Gb/s per user, which is over 1,000 times that of 4G [14]. 5G is not an extension of 3G and 4G; rather, it is an innovative web that includes a heterogeneous network, including 4G, Wi-Fi, millimeter wave, and other wireless access technologies [15]. The 5G networks offer a fully connected and interactive world with a variety of applications, including enhanced mobile broadband, machine-to-machine communications, artificial intelligence, and advanced digital services. By 2020, the 5G network will support 50 billion connected devices and 212 billion connected sensors and will enable access to 44 zettabytes (ZB) of data [16]. The huge network of devices connected to the Internet or the *Internet of Things* (IoT) may incorporate sensors to measure different variables in real time, including energy consumption, pressure, temperature, and many other economic, medical, or social indexes. Thanks to 5G, digital networks will connect billions of devices and sensors enabling advances in healthcare, education, resource management, transportation, agriculture, and many other areas [17]. For example, medical devices can reliably transmit the data about variables such as blood pressure, pulse, and breathing rate in near-real time to a health service provider, which can rapidly intervene in case of need. Road transport, train travel, and flights can become safer and more efficient, as connected vehicles and planes share information in real time with others. Similarly, manufacturing can be revolutionized with connected robots and sharing information about the different activities of the supply chain [18]. Buildings, bridges, and roads can be monitored continuously. Similarly, governments may use air-pollution monitoring data to control emissions.

The 5G systems include heterogeneous devices incorporating both low and high bandwidth. 5G is considered as a transformative system because it moves us from a user-centric world to the one based on machine-to-machine communications. This transformation and the ensuing IoT will connect these devices intelligently and lead to the commodification of information and intelligence [19]. The 5G will provide access to a wide range of services with increased resilience, continuity, and much higher resource efficiency, including a substantial decrease in energy consumption [20].

Blockchain

Blockchain can be defined as a distributed digital ledger that records transactions in a peer-to-peer network. The blockchain technology is a register that notifies and time—and date—stamps each exchange between each node in a block [21]. These characteristics enable several parties to use blockchain to engage in multiple transactions or exchanges without the presence of a third party. In other words, blockchain liberates users and transactions from the company of a trusted third party and creates immense opportunities for a distributed, secured disintermediation, organized in a peer-to-peer mode. The blockchain technology has the potential for innovation and the disruption of dominant economic models by creating an

Internet of transactions. While the idea of blockchain was appeared by the emergence of bitcoin, it can be used to create transactional highways for any peer-to-peer economic mode [21]. The concept of blockchain is very revolutionary because it can create a system based on trust, but without trusted third parties like banks, financial institutions, Airbnb, and Uber. Indeed, the alternative models to Uber may use the blockchain technologies to eliminate the intermediaries. The blockchain technologies allow the traceability, security, and transparency of each transaction. For example, cryptocurrencies such as bitcoin incorporate into the source code access to the past transactions relating to the unit of value, and at the same time, they protect the identity of the individuals associated with the transaction. As a result, the theft of a person's identity during the execution of a transaction becomes impossible [21]. Another advantage of the blockchain technology is its high speed of execution. The world of finance is currently testing the use of blockchain with a view to facilitating intermediation between banks, clearing houses, and central banks. The blockchain technology can be applied in various areas such as financial systems, sharing economy, smart contracts, including self-executing and autonomous algorithms, the digital vote, and the management of the logistics chain. The blockchain technology can transform the organization of transport, supply chain, advertising, energy production, and distribution sector, real estate market, insurance industry, and many other sectors by uniting the digital and physical worlds. Blockchain may help give objects an identity and full autonomy, thus creating opportunities for driverless cars and the IoT. In the field of Internet security, a startup called oneName is using the blockchain technology to make a unique digital identity, so the user can use this identity in multiple web-based platforms without memorizing different usernames and passwords. In the healthcare sector, another company BlockRX is using blockchain to digitize medical records and information about the patient that can be transferred more easily from one healthcare professional to another. The peer-to-peer insurance may create a revolution in the insurance industry by abolishing the current standards and the tripartite relationship between payers, insured parties, and insurers. Blockchain can be used in smart contracts where an agreement between two parties is digitalized, automated, and therefore self-executed. Ethereum, the second most popular cryptocurrency after bitcoin, is relying on smart contracts to give the various parties the assurance that, once the conditions have been fulfilled, the contract will be honored, with no possibility for fraud or interference with a third party [21].

Bluetooth 5.0

Bluetooth is a relatively old technology that has been developed more than two decades ago and is used for data transmission through radio waves. Bluetooth is a flexible technology, as it does not have any constraints to the type of the transmitted data, including photos, documents, music, and videos. However, one major limitation with Bluetooth has been the short range of data transmission that generally did not exceed 100 meters. Bluetooth 5.0 is the latest version of the Bluetooth wireless communication standard that offers significant improvements regarding the range, speed, and broadcasting capacity of data [22]. Bluetooth 5.0 offers 800 percent increase in data broadcasting capacity by doubling the speed and quadrupling the range of previous versions and maintains a very low power consumption. Therefore, the latest version of Bluetooth known as Bluetooth 5.0 can be used for wireless communication between various machine-to-machine communication and IoT devices [23]. Bluetooth technology will support the consumer adoption of the IoT, industrial automation, and the proliferation of dense sensor networks. By 2022, more than 50 billion connected devices worldwide will rely on Bluetooth 5.0 to connect and communicate [23].

Li-Fi

Li-Fi or light fidelity is a form of visible light communication that uses the visible light portion of the electromagnetic spectrum to provide local wireless communications at very high speeds. In other words, Li-Fi is a visible light communication system capable of transmitting data at high speeds over the visible light spectrum. As the visible light spectrum is 10,000 times larger than the radio waves, the Li-Fi technology can achieve Internet speeds of up to 224 GB per second that are much faster than the current standard Wi-Fi. The Li-Fi technology offers many advantages and peculiarities. For instance, while Wi-Fi works close to full capacity, Li-Fi has almost no limitations on capacity. As light cannot pass through walls, Li-Fi makes the transfer of data more secure than Wi-Fi and reduces the interference between multiple devices, and as a result, the transmitted data via Li-Fi cannot be hacked. Li-Fi offers many advantages, including working across higher bandwidth, working in areas susceptible to electromagnetic interference such as aircraft cabins and nuclear power plants. The Li-Fi technology may be applied in several areas such as the IoT, retail, construction, aviation, transportation, traffic management, and urban environments. Furthermore, future home and building automation are expected to be highly dependent on the Li-Fi technology for being secure and fast.

Quantum Computing

Quantum computing uses subatomic particles and quantum-mechanical phenomena such as superposition and entanglement to store data [24]. The current digital computing encodes data into binary digits (bits) that are always in one of two definite states (0 or 1), but quantum computation uses quantum bits that can hold much more complex information or even negative values [25]. In a conventional computer, bits are processed sequentially, but in quantum computation, qubits are entangled together, so changing the state of one qubit influences the state of others [25]. Unlike classical computing, quantum answers are probabilistic, and because of superposition and entanglement, multiple possible answers are considered in a given computation [25]. Therefore, quantum computers have a superior processing power than the current computers based on binary logic. Quantum computers are able to compute complex problems and offer novel possibilities. While classical or binary computers take more time for each variable added, quantum computers can rely on quantum bits to solve complex problems. Currently, quantum computing is more suitable for solving problems using three types of algorithms: optimization, sampling, and machine learning [25]. Full-scale quantum computers have not been developed yet, but the first basic systems threading together tens of quantum bits have been made available. Several national governments and military agencies are funding research to develop quantum computers for civilian, business, trade, environmental, and national security purposes. Many companies, including D-Wave, Google, Microsoft,

MIT Lincoln Laboratory, and Intelligence Advanced Research Projects Activity, are working on developing quantum hardware [25].

The applications of quantum computers are gaining acceptance in healthcare, manufacturing, supply chain management, purchasing, and procurement, production, and distribution. In investment and financial services, quantum computing could help determine attractive portfolios, given thousands of correlated assets [25]. Furthermore, quantum computing could be used to effectively identify fraud indicators. In healthcare, quantum computing can be used to predict the effects of potential therapeutic approaches and to optimize non-adverse effects. Lockheed Martin, one of the largest defense companies in the world, is using quantum computing to verify and validate aeronautics systems, design lifesaving drugs, and debug millions of lines of code [26]. In manufacturing, quantum computing could improve supply chain optimization problems in procurement, production, and distribution. Quantum computing can be useful in product optimization, advertising scheduling, and revenue maximization systems where hundreds of attributes about a consumer's preferences are collected. Quantum computing may strengthen the next generation of transport or logistics automation and remote sensor management.

Smart Dust

Smart dust is a network of micro-electro-mechanical devices, which includes a processing unit, some memory, and a radio chip, allowing them to communicate wirelessly with other smart dust devices within range [27]. Smart dust incorporates sensing, computing, wireless communication capabilities, and autonomous power supply at low cost. Furthermore, these smart dust devices are expected to be so small and light that they can remain suspended in the environment like ordinary dust particles [28]. Because of these features, smart dust can be used to scrutinize the environment without affecting the natural processes. By collecting data in real time via miniaturized low-power sensors and wireless networks, smart dust will transform our understanding of the environment. Currently, the size of smart dust particles is about five cubic millimeters, but the size will continue to become smaller. The University of California at Berkeley's Smart Dust research team estimates that they can fit in the necessary sensing, communication, and computing hardware, with a power supply, in a volume no more than a few cubic millimeters [28]. Therefore, the future models of smart dust are expected to be small enough to remain suspended in air and communicate for a long period, sometimes for many years. The smart dust technology is in its infancy, but it has the potential to be applied in different areas, including security, military, traffic management, construction, mining, agriculture, and urban planning. The smart dust technology can allow continuous real-time monitoring of industrial and urban projects and structures. The data gathered on environmental, biological, and structural variables may help to improve the efficiency of global resource use. The experiments in California showed that the smart dust technology can be used by military and law enforcement personnel to monitor movement in the region [28]. Some examples of the smart dust technology include arranging defense networks by unmanned aerial vehicles, tracking the movements of birds, small animals, and insects, monitoring environmental conditions, managing inventory, and monitoring product quality [29].

The development of smart dust technology increases some concerns about privacy and security issues. The minuscule smart dust sensors could be used for mischievous, illegal, or unethical purposes. For example, the smart dust technology can be used for industrial espionage or for monitoring people without their knowledge. As smart dust technology becomes smaller, cheaper, and more powerful, the risks and concerns associated with the misuse of this technology will grow exponentially. One major concern is that once the smart dust networks are scattered, they are not easily retrieved, and they may involve serious environmental polluting effects.

Interfaces and Visualization

Deep Mapping

Deep mapping is an emerging technology that refers to a map incorporating various types of data within a geographic information system (GIS) environment [36]. Thus, deep mapping investigates the spatial location and systematizes different levels of information into conceptions using three-dimensional scenes. Deep mapping collects data from many sources, including remote sensor networks, aerial and satellite imagery, crowdsourcing, smartphones, and on-site mapping vehicles. The deep maps may contain rich and valuable information about a location regarding health, education, demographics, physical variables, air pollution, driving conditions, commercial and business issues, and many other factors. Deep mapping can be combined with surveillance devices to provide a richer visualization of a location. By offering both historical and real-time information about each particular location in one single interface, deep mapping can facilitate planning and decision-making in many areas such as construction, traffic control, agriculture, and business activities. For instance, Google's Ground Truth is an ongoing project that combines data from governments and other organizations with the data it gathers itself through satellite imagery [37].

Mixed Reality

The concept of mixed reality is an emerging trend in information technology and refers to the integration of the physical and digital worlds. Mixed reality is the result of recent progress in computer vision, graphical processing power, sensors, display technology, mobile network capacity, and input systems. Unlike virtual reality and augmented reality, mixed reality does not immerse any content onto the real world; rather, it uses transparent lenses to make virtual objects both appear and interact with real ones. The mixed reality technological features provide virtual objects with a realistic sense of touch and change how people access information, share experiences, and provide feedback. Therefore, the mixed reality is expected to drastically change the relationships between human, computer, and physical environment. The combination of computer processing, human input, and environmental input creates mixed reality experiences. For instance, movement in the physical space can be translated into movement in the digital world and vice versa. Indeed, mixed reality can be positioned between augmented reality and virtual reality. The current augmented reality and virtual reality offerings represent a very small part of this spectrum and do not allow blending digital representations of people, places, and things with the real world. The windows mixed reality devices are either holographic or immersive. The holographic devices can place digital content in the real world as if it were there, whereas the immersive devices can hide or change the physical world and replace it with a digital experience. Fragments and RoboRaid are immersive devices that use the user's physical environment like walls, floors, and furniture to place digital content in the world. Mixed reality can unleash unbelievable possibilities beyond our imagination. Due to its spatial technology, mixed reality will have major applications and implications in the areas such as design, architecture, and construction. For example, Microsoft's HoloLens enables users to view and interact with scalable, photorealistic, and responsive 3D holograms overlaid on the user's visual field. Some businesses are using mixed reality technology to inspect three-dimensional renderings of site plans prior to construction.

Multi-Sensory Interfaces

Multi-sensory interfaces are emerging technologies that allow communication between humans and machines through a wide range of senses, eye or body movements, speech, and gestures. Due to their ease of use, multi-sensory interfaces are expected to replace conventional computer control systems such as keyboard and mouse. The integration of speech and other forms of conversational interfaces may allow real-time cross-language communications in a near future. Developments in mixed reality and virtual reality will require a new generation of user interfaces and experiences. Multi-sensory interfaces process multiple inputs across multiple devices to deliver contextual, connected, and viral experiences; they use all senses to capture information; and they do not ask for any information they should already know. They can rely on the previous data, and they continue to learn from their user's behaviors [38]. For instance, Samsung Inc. is developing a blink-detecting contact lens equipped with a display, camera, antenna, and movement sensors that can project an image directly onto the eye's retina.

Materials

Nanomaterials

Nanotechnology is a fast growing area that is concerned with the production of very small particles or nanomaterials. A nanometer is one billionth of a meter, and nanomaterials are less than 100 nanometers.

Nanotechnology relies on microscopic processing techniques to produce various materials and components. Generally, there are two methods to produce nanomaterials. In the top-down method, small components are produced using larger parts of the material. In the bottom-up method, nanomaterials are produced from molecules or atoms. In nanotechnology, normal rules of physics and chemistry no longer apply, and many materials may show unique properties. For instance, they may become very much stronger, more conductive, or reactive [39]. One substantial property of nanoparticles is the massive surface area that makes them different from other materials [40]. Because of their essential characteristics, such as strength, lightweight, and insulating properties, nanomaterials have widespread applications in many industries, including agriculture and food, energy production and efficiency, automotive industry, cosmetics, medical appliances and drugs, household appliances, computers, and weapons [41]. There are many possible applications of nanomaterials in building corrosion-free steel, low-energy LEDs, and ultra-thin PV cells. Nanomaterials such as graphene could be used in water purification technology to improve access to clean drinking water. Nontechnology has various applications in the field of electronics. For instance, nontechnology is used in the miniaturized products to make high-purity materials with better thermal conductivity. Furthermore, nanomaterials are used to produce long-lasting and durable interconnections. Because of their physical characteristics, nanomaterials are used in developing super-capacitors that have a large capacity compared with normal capacitors.

Nanotechnology can be used to produce effective insulation materials for homes and offices. High-energy density batteries, heating, and cooling bills, and cutting tools are other areas of nanomaterial applications. Nanoparticles can be used in medicine to selectively deliver drugs to specific cells. This method reduces the overall drug consumption and side-effects by placing the active agent in the morbid region [42]. Nanotechnology may be applied in all stages of food preparation, including production, processing, safety, and packaging. Currently, nanoparticles are used to create new food products. By adding nanoparticles to a polymer, a nanocomposite is formed that is much more transparent than a polymer containing micron particles, which is opaque. In energy production, nanotechnology offers a practical alternative to non-renewable fossil-fuel consumption by producing cheaper, cleaner, and more efficient and renewable energies. Nanotechnology is still in its infancy, and many of its applications are under development.

Programmable Materials

Programmable materials can change their physical properties such as shape, density, conductivity, and optical properties in a programmable way depending on user input or self-sufficient sensing [42]. In other words, programmable materials refer to a form of controlled and shape-shifting matter that can transition from their current shape into the desired shape with complete reversibility [43]. There are two primary approaches to programmable matter: bottom-up attempts to change the behavior of materials at the atomic or molecular level and top-down approaches to creating miniature robotic systems to form a larger item [44]. Programmable materials could drastically change our understanding of the matter, and naturally, could have major implications for all aspects of our lives. The idea of programmable materials implies that the matter can be reused infinitely for different purposes. Programmed materials could bring a new generation of structures that respond dynamically and automatically to their environment. Applications of programmable materials could include architecture, infrastructure, production lines, construction, and operation. Programmable materials can be used in paintable displays, shape-changing robots and tools, rapid prototyping, and sculpture-based haptic interfaces. For instance, researchers at the MIT are working on a project to build shape-shifting carbon fiber in a racing car spoiler. The spoiler reacts to environmental change, morphing into its most efficient shape and improving the car's performance. The MIT Media Lab recently showed the latest version of Transform, which is a form of dynamic furniture that can turn digital information into three-dimensional shapes. The Transform dynamic furniture responds to hand movements to change its shape.

Bio-Based Materials

The term *bio-based material* refers to a wide range of substances such as chemicals, natural fibers, plastics, concrete, wood, composites, and final products. Bio-based materials are substances derived from living organisms. The production of bio-based materials does not rely on the extraction and emission of fossil carbon; instead, it uses feedstock that contains biogenic carbon. The feedstock may include agricultural crops, residues, and organic waste streams, wood, microorganisms, and animal products [45]. Bio-based materials offer sustainable alternatives to fossil-based materials, as they are often biodegradable and use low-energy production routes. The production of bio-based materials smartly uses biomass and contributes positively to savings in greenhouse gas emissions, toxicity, and waste reduction [46]. Therefore, the bio-based materials industry is attractive to policymakers, as it is associated with sustainable development, environmental protection, and the circular economy [47]. Furthermore, the bio-based materials industry offers exciting opportunities to rural areas in terms of economic development and job creation [48]. Due to their environmental benefits, bio-based materials have various applications. The bio-based materials industry may grow by 300 percent in the next four years. Construction, furniture, packaging, and manufacturing industries are likely to adopt bio-based materials. The attractiveness of bio-based materials will encourage researchers and engineers to accelerate innovation. For instance, researchers at the Wageningen Institute in the Netherlands have developed bioplastics for packaging, casings for consumer electronics, textiles, and parts for the automotive industry. Furthermore, they are developing inks, coatings, paper, cardboard, construction materials from biomasses [49].

Energy and Resources

Foam Batteries

Batteries are big businesses, as they are used in various devices from computers and tablets to cars and wearables. The conventional batteries are made up of two-dimensional surfaces that limit the direction and speed at which energy can flow. As a result, the existing batteries take a long time to charge, lose energy rapidly, and require frequent replacement. Prieto, an innovative startup, is introducing the new batteries produced with a copper foam substrate that is approximately 98 percent air or void space [29]. Due to an increase in the surface area of approximately 60 times, the foam battery is expected to have much higher power densities. The foam battery will be customizable and can be optimized for either power density or energy density [30]. Furthermore, the foam battery technology promises to be cost-effective to manufacture and fast to charge. In addition, the foam batteries are smaller, lighter, safer, and less toxic than traditional 2D batteries. Some large companies in the consumer electronics sector such as Apple, LG, and Nokia, have shown a growing interest in the new battery technology [29]. The foam batteries can be shaped to fit spaces that are inaccessible to traditional batteries in a safer and less expensive way. Because of its unique design, the foam battery can be used in wearables and tablets without compromising energy and power [30]. Furthermore, the foam battery technology can be used to build novel devices with military and industrial applications. In the transport sector, the foam battery technology is expected to be a viable option by offering improved efficiency, higher safety, and lower cost. Over time, the foam technology could provide energy storage solutions for grid-scale applications [29].

Fusion Reactors

In a fusion process, power is generated by using nuclear fusion reactions. During the process, two lighter atomic nuclei combine to form a heavier nucleus, and at the same time, they release large amounts of energy that can be harnessed to produce electricity. The fusion process in reactors is similar to what happens in stars like the sun. The fusion releases massive amounts of energy about one million times more powerful than a chemical reaction, and 3 to 4 times more powerful than a conventional fission nuclear reaction. Fusion seems more advantageous than fission because it is safer and produces more energy and less waste and radioactivity. Fusion reactors could provide clean energy with no long-lasting radioactive waste. The vast amount of energy produced by fusion reactors can change the transport and other energy-intensive industries and replace fossil fuels. The major barriers to fusion power are fuel and a highly confined environment with a high temperature and pressure. Lockheed Martin, a giant defense firm, is working on the use of magnetic field pressure to make a fusion reactor that is 10 times smaller than other prototypes. The use of magnetic field pressure may be effective in managing extremely high temperatures during the fusion process [28].

Transparent Solar Panels

Researchers at Michigan State University invented a transparent luminescent solar panel in 2014 [31]. Transparent solar panels use organic materials to absorb light wavelengths that are invisible to the human eye. Currently, the main obstacle to the widespread use of conventional photovoltaic panels is their appearance [32]. Therefore, the transparency of solar panels is a significant game-changer because the transparent panels could replace conventional window glasses. Urban areas that do not have enough rooftop space will be able to transform their glass windows into energy-producing panels. Commercial buildings have many windows, which means huge energy generation with solar panels [32]. In addition, the new solar panels can come in colorful semi-transparent devices, which designers and architects can use to design or decorate building [29]. In addition, transparent materials can be used on car windows, cell phones, or other devices with a clear surface and transform any surface into an energy-producing system. It is estimated that, by using invisible solar panels, a skyscraper could provide more than a quarter of the building's energy needs [33]. The widespread adoption of such panels can meet U.S. electricity demand and significantly reduce the use of other energy resources like fossil fuels. Transparent solar technologies could supply some 40 percent of energy demand in the United States in the next decade. Although the cost of developing transparent panels remains high and their energy output is still limited, their prospective extensive application is appealing to scientists and investors.

Pollution Digesters

With increasing levels of environmental pollution, the reduction of pollutants is becoming a serious challenge for many countries across the world. The pollution digestion technologies have been considered as solutions to the deteriorating air quality and environmental pollution, particularly in urban areas. Pollution digesters could include a wide range of methods, including anaerobic, large-scale air ionizers, and photocatalytically active substances. In the anaerobic digestion, organic matter is broken down into smaller particles by reactions in the absence of oxygen [34]. An anaerobic digester can be designed to treat different waste flows, for example, municipal solid waste, municipal organic waste, industrial waste, or sludge from a wastewater treatment plant [35]. The pollution digestion technologies can be used to remove, filter, and transform airborne pollutants, and thus improve air quality. Pollution digesters may be installed in building facades or across the urban areas to improve air pollution. As the quality of air, particularly in Asia and South America, continues to deteriorate, there is a growing interest from business and scientific communities in developing more efficient pollution digesters. For instance, Photoment is a powder-like substance that is photocatalytically active and reacts with sunlight to transform toxic airborne nitrous oxide into non-toxic nitrates that are not harmful to the environment or human health and is washed away by rain. Photoment can be added to the concrete paving surfaces in urban areas to reduce the number of airborne pollutants.

References

[1]   Sabhikhi, A. 2018. "10 Questions about Augmented Intelligence." *Cognitive Scale*. https://cognitivescale.com/augmented-intelligence-you-can-trust/

[2]   Kockelman, K. 2017. "An Assessment of Autonomous Vehicles: Traffic Impacts and Infrastructure Needs--Final Report." *Center for Transportation Research*. The University of Texas at Austin.

[3]   Smith, B.W., and J. Svensson. 2015. *Automated and Autonomous Driving: Regulation under Uncertainty.*

[4]   Hedlund, J. 2017. "Autonomous Vehicles Meet Human Drivers: Traffic Safety Issues for States." *Spotlight on Highway Safety*. Governors Highway Safety Association.

[5]   Ford. 2016. "Ford Targets Fully Autonomous Vehicle for Ride Sharing in 2021; Invests in New Tech Companies, Doubles Silicon Valley Team." Press release August 16, 2016. https://media.ford.com/content/fordmedia/fna/us/en/news/2016/08/16/ford-targets-fullyautonomous-vehicle-for-ride-sharing-in-2021.html

[6]   Autonomous Vehicles Readiness Index, Assessing countries' openness and preparedness for autonomous vehicles. https://assets.kpmg.com/

content/dam/kpmg/nl/pdf/2018/sector/automotive/autonomous-vehicles-readiness-index.pdf

[7] Angerholzer III, M., D. Mahaffee, M. Vale, J. Kitfield, and H. Renner. 2017. *The Autonomous Vehicle Revolution: Fostering Innovation with Smart Regulation.*

[8] Autonomous Vehicles Considerations for Personal and Commercial Lines Insurers. 2016. https://munichre.com/site/mram-mobile/get/documents_ E706434935/mram/assetpool.mr_america/PDFs/3_Publications/ Autonomous_Vehicles.pdf

[9] Anderson, J.M., K. Nidhi, K.D. Stanley, P. Sorensen, C. Samaras, and O.A. Oluwatola. 2014. *Autonomous Vehicle Technology: A Guide for Policymakers.* Rand Corporation.

[10] Henaghan, J. 2018. "Preparing Communities for Autonomous Vehicles." https://planning-org-uploaded-media.s3.amazonaws.com/document/ Autonomous-Vehicles-Symposium-Report.pdf

[11] Kuzma, J., S. O'Sullivan, T.W. Philippe, J.W. Koehler, and R.S. Coronel. 2017. "Commercialization Strategy in Managing Online Presence in the Unmanned Aerial Vehicle Industry." *International Journal of Business Strategy* 17, no. 1, pp. 59–68.

[12] www.PassengerDrone.com

[13] Undertaking, S.J. 2016. *European Drones Outlook Study-Unlocking the Value for Europe.* SESAR, Brussels.

[14] Starkloff, E. 2015. "The Future of 5G: The Internet for Everyone and Everything." *Business 2 Community Magazine* 21.

[15] West, D.M. 2016. "How 5G Technology Enables the Health Internet of Things." *Brookings Center for Technology Innovation* 3, pp. 1–20.

[16] Numbers cited in MacGillivray, C. 2013. "The Internet of Things Is Poised to Change Everything, Says IDC." *Business Wire*, October 3, 2013; and McLellan, C. 2015. "The Internet of Things and Big Data." *ZDNet*, March 2, 2015.

[17] King, I. "5G Networks Will Do Much More Than Stream Better Cat Videos." *Bloomberg News*, May 2, 2016.

[18] Davies, R. 2016. "5G Network Technology: Putting Europe at the Leading Edge." *EPRS, European Parliamentary Research Service, Members' Research Service.*

[19] King, I. "5G Networks Will Do Much More Than Stream Better Cat Videos." *Bloomberg News*, May 2, 2016.

[20] 5G Infrastructure Association. 2015. *The 5G Infrastructure Public Private Partnership: The Next Generation of Communication Networks and Services.*

[21] Peters, G.W., and E. Panayi. 2016. "Understanding Modern Banking Ledgers through Blockchain Technologies: Future of Transaction Processing

and Smart Contracts on the Internet of Money." In *Banking Beyond Banks and Money*, 239–78. Springer, Cham.

[22] Collotta, M., G. Pau, T. Talty, and O.K. Tonguz. 2017. *Bluetooth 5: A Concrete Step Forward Towards the IoT*. ArXiv preprint arXiv: 1711.00257.

[23] Chang, K.H. 2014. "Bluetooth: A Viable Solution for IoT? [Industry Perspectives]." *IEEE Wireless Communications* 21, no. 6, pp. 6–7.

[24] Gershenfeld, N., and I.L. Chuang. June 1998. "Quantum Computing with Molecules (PDF)." *Scientific American*.

[25] Accenture. 2018. "Innovating with Quantum Computing Enterprise Experimentation Provides View into Future of Computing." https://accenture.com/t00010101T000000__w__/br-pt/_acnmedia/PDF-45/Accenture-Innovating-Quantum-Computing-Novo.pdf

[26] Srivastava, R., I. Choi, T. Cook, and N.U.E. Team. 2016. *The Commercial Prospects for Quantum Computing. Networked Quantum Information Technologies*.

[27] Arief, B., P. Blythe, and A. Tully. 2013. *Using Smart Dust in Transport Domain*.

[28] Azodolmolky, S., P. Wieder, and R. Yahyapour. 2013. "Cloud computing Networking: Challenges and Opportunities for Innovations." *IEEE Communications Magazine* 51, no. 7, pp. 54–62.

[29] Chen, C.C., L. Dou, R. Zhu, C.H. Chung, T.B. Song, Y.B. Zheng, and Y. Yang. 2012. "Visibly Transparent Polymer Solar Cells Produced by Solution Processing." *Acs Nano* 6, no. 8, pp. 7185–90.

[30] https://prietobattery.com

[31] "This Full Transparent Solar Cell Could Make Every Screen a Power Source." *Extreme Tech*. April 20, 2015. http://extremetech.com/extreme/188667-a-fully-transparent-solar-cell-that-could-make-every-window-and-screen-a-power-source (accessed December 31, 2016).

[32] "Solar Energy That Doesn't Block the View." Michigan State University, August 19, 2014. (accessed October 29, 2016)

[33] Chang, S.Y., P. Cheng, G. Li, and Y. Yang. 2018. "Transparent Polymer Photovoltaics for Solar Energy Harvesting and Beyond." *Joule* 2, no. 6, pp. 1039–54.

[34] Adekunle, K.F., and J.A. Okolie. 2015. "A Review of Biochemical Process of Anaerobic Digestion." *Advances in Bioscience and Biotechnology Ad-Vances in Bioscience and Biotechnology* 6, no. 6, pp. 205–12. http://doi.org/10.4236/abb.2015.63020

[35] Arivalagan, K., S. Ravichandran, K. Rangasamy, and E. Karthikeyan. 2011. "Nanomaterials and Its Potential Applications." *Int. J. ChemTech Res* 3, no. 2, pp. 534–38.

[36] Bodenhamer, D.J., J. Corrigan, and T.M. Harris, eds. 2015. "Deep Maps and Spatial Narratives." *Indiana University Press.*

[37] https://techcrunch.com/2014/09/03/googles-ground-truth-initiative-for-building-more-accurate-maps-now-covers-50-countries/

[38] Christophe Coenraets and James Ward. 2015. Principles of Multi-Sensory Applications, available at: https://multisensory.github.io/

[39] Roco, M.C., C.A. Mirkin, and M.C. Hersam. 2011. *Nanotechnology Research Directions for Societal Needs in 2020: Summary of International Study.*

[40] Shaffer, M.S., and A.H. Windle. 1999. *Advanced Materials* 11, p. 937.

[41] Varma, R.S., R.K. Saini, and R. Dahiya. 1997. "Active Manganese Dioxide on Silica: Oxidation of Alcohols under Solvent-Free Conditions Using Microwaves." *Tetrahedron letters* 38, no. 45, pp. 7823–24.

[42] Knaian, A.N. 2008. *Design of Programmable Matter.* Doctoral [dissertation], Massachusetts Institute of Technology.

[43] Amend, J.R., and H. Lipson. 2009. "Shape-Shifting Materials for Programmable Structures." In *International Conference on Ubiquitous Computing: Workshop on Architectural Robotics.*

[44] Kirby, B.T., B. Aksak, J.D. Campbell, J.F. Hoburg, T.C. Mowry, P. Pillai, and S.C. Goldstein. 2007. "A Modular Robotic System Using Magnetic Force Effectors." *Proc. IROS* 2007, *IEEE Comp. Soc. Press*, pp. 2787–93.

[45] Broeren, M.L.M. 2018. *Sustainable Bio-Based Materials-Application and Evaluation of Environmental Impact Assessment Methods.* Utrecht University.

[46] Schmidt, O., S. Padel, and L. Levidow. 2012. "The Bio-Economy Concept and Knowledge Base in Public Goods and Farmer Perspective." *Bio-Based and Applied Economics* 1, no. 1, pp. 47–63.

[47] Broeren, M.L.M. 2018. *Sustainable Bio-Based Materials-Application and Evaluation of Environmental Impact Assessment Methods.* Utrecht University.

[48] van der Meer, Y. 2017. *Sustainable Bio-Based Materials: Opportunities and Challenges.*

[49] https://wur.nl/en/About-Wageningen.htm

About the Author

Dr. Yeganeh is a professor of international management at Winona State University in Minnesota. He is a multidisciplinary scholar who earned his MBA, MSc, and PhD from Université Laval in Quebec, Canada. His research focuses on global business and cross-cultural management. His scholarly research has appeared in various journals such as *Journal of International Management, Competiveness Review, International Journal of Human Resource Management, Journal of East-West Business, and Cross-Cultural Management.*

Index

OTHER TITLES IN THE INTERNATIONAL BUSINESS COLLECTION

Tamer Cavusgil, Georgia State; Michael Czinkota, Georgetown; and Gary Knight, Willamette University, Editors

Announcing the Business Expert Press Digital Library

Concise e-books business students need for classroom and research

This book can also be purchased in an e-book collection by your library as

- a one-time purchase,
- that is owned forever,
- allows for simultaneous readers,
- has no restrictions on printing, and
- can be downloaded as PDFs from within the library community.

Our digital library collections are a great solution to beat the rising cost of textbooks. E-books can be loaded into their course management systems or onto student's e-book readers.
The **Business Expert Press** digital libraries are very affordable, with no obligation to buy in future years. For more information, please visit **www.businessexpertpress.com/librarians**. To set up a trial in the United States, please email **sales@businessexpertpress.com**.